Writing
for
Profit

John Wade

Writing
for
Profit

John Wade

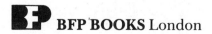

BFP BOOKS London

© 1986 BFP Books

First Edition 1986

British Library Cataloguing in Publication Data:

Wade, John, *1945–*
    Writing for profit.
    1. Authorship
    I. Title
    808'.02   PN145
    ISBN 0-907297-08-0

Published by BFP Books (Lyndtree Ltd), Focus House, 497 Green Lanes, London N13 4BP, and printed in Great Britain by A. Wheaton & Co. Ltd., Exeter.

CONTENTS

INTRODUCTION

"No man but a blockhead ever wrote, except for money."
—Dr. Samuel Johnson

There was a time, during the preparation of this book, when I toyed with the idea of calling it "How To Be a Hack". For those unfamiliar with the word, it is derived from its use in the world of horses, in which a hack is one such animal that is let out for hire. It especially refers to a poor quality of saddle horse and, from there, the word has found itself further applied to a person considered to be a drudge or one who is generally overworked. In this human rather than equine context, the word *hack* gets defined more particularly as one who produces inferior and badly-paid literary work. To be a hack, then, might not be considered the best job in town.

Allow me to disagree. First with the definition of the word, then with its application to the world of commercial writing. In my book, a hack is an honoured profession, one that contains men and woman who have learnt the art of turning out words quickly, accurately and aimed unerringly at their market; writers who can research a subject and write about it for one market, then turn it around, adapt it and aim it at another market; those who can come up with a good idea to begin with, then milk that idea for all its worth to get the most from it. The words they write are not designed, as those in a Shakespeare sonnet might be, to thrill, excite or even generate in the reader admiration for the writer; they are designed to bring information and entertainment to people who want certain facts — or even fiction — presented in a way that is easy to digest and relevant to their own way of life.

We hear about Fleet Street Hacks. We even hear people talk in derogatory terms about the men and woman who fill our morning tabloids with words. But the fact is that newspapers are in business to make money for their proprietors. To do that, they must keep selling, taking every opportunity to beat the opposition. The words in a newspaper are designed to be read, and in the most cases, they *are* read — avidly. They supply a specific need. The people who produce them are extremely professional writers who know exactly the style that is guaranteed to make their newspapers successful. If you want a ready-made exercise in concise writing, do no more than try to emulate the style you've seen in your morning paper. In there, on every page, reporters are telling complete stories on every subject under the sun, often in no more than a couple of hundred words. There are few places where you'll see a more professional approach to commercial writing. The standard might not be literary in the way a book by Dickens is literary, but neither is it in any way inferior. It's just different, that's all. And the person who wrote it isn't badly paid either!

What we're dealing with here, then, is ways in which you can learn to write professionally and make money from what you write. If that means being a hack, then so be it. No one is pretending that this book is going to turn you into a literary genius, or that it will make you a vast fortune. There are books around that purport to do that, explaining how you can become a best-selling novelist overnight, going on to sell the film rights of your first novel and ending up sipping champagne on your own yacht. It's possible, believe me, it *is* possible — but it's improbable. There are first-time novelists who make it big the first time round. But for every one who succeeds in this way, there are a million who fail. What I want to do, throughout the pages of this book, is to be honest with you and to talk practically.

How this book can help

Unless you are that one in a million with a God-given talent for writing, who gets his or her book to the right people at the right time, you're not going to strike it rich by this time next week. But, given time, perseverance and the ability to learn a few simple rules, I am going to teach you how to write the sort of words that sell. Then I'll tell you where to sell them and how to go about the actual sale. Using the information contained in this book, even if you have never written more than a letter home to your mum in the past, you should be able to learn how to write saleable material. The sort of money you can earn at this type of writing varies from a nice little second income to a well-paid, full-time job, depending on how much time and effort you are prepared to put in. It won't make you a millionaire, but it might easily lead you to earning a good deal more than you might from most regular occupations. And it'll be a lot more fun too!

There's nothing mysterious about commercial writing. It's a job like any other. Okay, so a certain amount of talent helps, and anyone who is what we might term a naturally-talented writer will probably make it in the end without any help. But commercial writing for no reason other than the profit it generates is a craft, and one that can be learnt in the same way as you learnt how to ride a bike or cook a meal.

If you regularly read books that set out to teach you the rudiments of any particular subject, you might already have noticed one fairly important difference between this and the others: the fact that it is written in the first person. This is *me*, sitting here talking to you, not some nebulous third-person author, dispensing information anonymously. Mine isn't the usual way to write books of instruction (indeed, it isn't even the way that *I've* written other books in other fields), but I believe it to be the right way this time round. It's something that I thought long and hard about even before I put pen to paper, or to be more precise, finger to word processor — of which, more later.

The reason I decided on this style is very simple. I'm out to teach you how to write for profit. It's something I know about because it's the way I earn my living. My own experiences over the years are going to be of benefit to you, and writing the book in this way, I'll be able to give you those experiences in a more personal and, ultimately, more meaningful way. Telling you how *I* learnt my craft, will help *you* learn yours. Owning up to some of the mistakes I made along the way should help prevent you from doing the same thing. And if I can throw in a little anecdote here and there to make the point even more clear, so much the better. All of that is difficult to do, if I am writing in the third person.

The first job I had, that in any way concerned the written word, was as a general news reporter on a local newspaper. The total staff consisted of an editor, two reporters, a sports writer, a part-time photographer and a lady downstairs who took the adverts. The building we were in was beside a railway line. Every time a train went past, cups rattled along desks and fell on the floor. The sports writer had a typewriter without a "W" or "D" on it and he had to write those letters in by hand every time he took a sheet of paper out of his machine. You probably have some idea of the kind of outfit I'm talking about.

It was a lousy paper, but it was a great training ground, and the man who made it great was the editor. He taught me to write commercially and much of what he told me, in his own individual and sometimes eccentric way, is still with me today.

"I'm going to take a hammer to this sentence and break it up into small bits," he'd say as he gleefully attacked my latest masterpiece with a great thick pencil.

If he heard me on the phone, saying something like, "I don't suppose you could tell me . . ." he would thunder across the office, "Don't ask negative questions", and I'd have to adjust my question to something more positive, saying, "Will you please tell me now . . ."

One day, tired of my continued misspelling of a certain word, he wrote the correct spelling on a piece of cardboard 2ft. long and nailed it to my desk with a six inch nail.

Experiences like those stay with you. Today, I rarely write long, convoluted copy. I break everything down into small, easy-to-read and easy-to-understand sentences. I don't ask negative questions when I'm interviewing. And I never misspell that particular word.

This book isn't meant to be the story of my life, but suffice to say that since those days, I have worked on several newspapers in the capacity of reporter, feature writer, sub-editor and deputy editor, spent a year earning my living writing fiction, worked for seven years as editor of a national photographic magazine and, today, happily work for myself, writing magazine articles, books, brochures, leaflets, advertising copy and technical material for various clients in the photographic manufacturing and distribution business. I also take pictures to illustrate my words. These are my qualifications for telling you how to write and make money from what you've written.

The markets

We'll start by looking at the actual hardware you need to be a successful writer, then move straight on to perhaps the most lucrative market of all for the beginner, that of magazines. We'll look at what's available, how to choose the right one for your needs and how to analyse it to find out what to write. Then we'll move on to the individual *types* of magazines with an in-depth look at what each of the more popular categories demand. Having found our market, we'll deal with methods of researching magazine articles, before dealing in detail with how to get the actual words down on paper.

From magazines we'll move to newspapers, looking at the difference between the two markets and how you can supply exactly what's needed.

Books come next. Not fiction, because non-fiction is much easier to get published and, remember, I want to deal here with what is truly *practical* for the newcomer to writing, rather than try to sell you a dream.

What *is* practical, is the way you can considerably increase your chances of success in the writing world by adding pictures to your words. You don't have to be a professional photographer to take the type of pictures that sell as article illustrations, and you don't need a vast knowledge of photography either. Today's cameras take care of the technology, leaving you to concentrate on the subject. In this section, I'll be telling you what sort of camera the non-photographer can handle easily, and I'll give you some tips on how to take the sort of pictures that sell.

Although I don't recommend the newcomer to writing to try his or her hand at a novel, there is a market for fiction that is worth looking into. Short stories are still bought by a lot of different types of publication and, if you can learn to write a magazine article, you can learn to write a short story. In that field, we'll be examining how to make a start, how to plot a story and then taking a more detailed look at three specific types of short story that regularly make sales for writers, amateur and professional alike.

Having found your market and written your copy, you'll need to know something about how best to present it. That's covered next, together with advice on how to make contact with an editor, how to ensure you get paid the right amount and how to handle the fees you receive.

Finally, if you fail to sell your work after all the advice you've been given, we'll discuss ways of looking at things anew, how to analyse where you might have gone wrong and, more to the point, how to put it right.

Chances of success

Writing is uncomfortably like a drug at times. Once you start, and once you get your first taste of success, it's very difficult to stop. Yet anyone who has been at it for a while will tell you that there are times when it can be equally difficult to start. As much as you want to *be* writing, you find yourself not wanting to *begin* writing. If that sounds like double-dutch, all I can say is, wait until you have been writing seriously for a while, and I'll bet you anything you like that you'll have cause to look back on these remarks and smile.

Writing, it has been observed, is mainly a matter of application — primarily the application of the backside to the chair. So if you're sitting comfortably, we'll begin . . .

THE TOOLS OF THE TRADE

**"The biggest obstacle to professional writing today
is the necessity for changing a typewriter ribbon."**
— Robert Benchley

Here is all the equipment you need to be a successful writer: a box of paper and a reasonably sharp pencil. That's all you *need*, but undoubtedly the addition of a few other items of hardware will not only make life easier, it will also make you more efficient, give your work more authority and, ultimately, give you a better chance of selling your writing.

The most obvious, and probably the most important, piece of equipment you can invest in is a typewriter of some sort. Immediately, I hear the cry go up across the land: "Typewriter? I can't type. It needs years of training to become a fast and accurate typist." Absolutely right. But we're not talking about becoming a *typist*. We're talking about becoming a *writer*. A typist is someone who looks at notes or listens to a dictating machine and turns it all into neat, accurate words on the page, fingers flying over the keyboard, each one assigned to its own set of keys, never missing a beat and without even the necessity of looking at the machine. Some writers are like that too. But mostly, they're the ones who sit, staring at the keyboard rather than the paper, using two fingers and making mistakes. Generally speaking, though, they're just as fast, even if they're not as accurate, and even if their style of typing makes trained typists cringe.

In a moment, we'll look at the different types of machine that are available, but first let's look at a few points that are general to all models. If you already know something about the rudiments of typing, then this next section is going to be pretty obvious, so by all means skip it. But if you've never typed or even looked seriously at a typewriter, then you might find some tips here that will prove invaluable.

Typing for non-typists

The keys on a typewriter are not arranged in alphabetical order. To the newcomer, trying to find his or her way around the keyboard for the first time, that might seem a little strange. But there is a good reason for it. Put your hands out in front of you, palms facing away. The digits that are easiest for you to use are most probably the thumb, first and second finger of each hand. The third and fourth fingers are a little weaker. Now place your hands over a typewriter keyboard. You'll find the letters you use the most situated around the centre, falling under your strongest fingers, while those at the outside edges of the keyboard are the letters you use to a lesser extent. So the keyboard of a typewriter is arranged, basically, around three rows of letters that read,

QWERTYUIOP

ASDFGHJKL

ZXCVBNM

The vast majority of machines also have a fourth row of figures above the letters that reads,

1234567890

Other keys to the sides will contain punctuation, fractions and the like, while the long key that travels right across the bottom is the space bar.

Typing normally, all the letters will be printed in the lower case—what we called "small letters" when we were at school. Pressing the key marked *shift* while you press any of the letter keys, prints in capitals. Pressing the *shift lock* keeps the shift down until you press the key again to release it, for times when you want to stay in capitals.

Keys other than those with straightforward letters on them usually contain two symbols. The figure 2, for instance, will probably have a double quote sign over it. In all cases, typing normally produces the lower symbol, while typing with the shift key produces the upper one.

There are several controls which affect the way the words fall on the paper. One is the margin, another is the tab. The margin controls the width of the line. You set the left margin to control at which point you wish every line to begin and the right one to control where it should end. There is usually some kind of audible device built into the machine to tell you when you are approaching the end of each line. The tab control—short for "tabulator"—is for those times when you want certain items to appear at the same place in each line. You set it in advance at the required key points, after which merely pressing the tab key will take you straight to each pre-set place on the line. It is most useful for preparing columns of figures, when you want each to fall accurately under the one above, but for our purposes, its most useful function is for starting paragraphs. Set the tab five spaces in from the left margin, then, each time you press the key, you'll be in just the right place to begin an indented line for a new paragraph. A third aspect that concerns you is the line space control. This automatically adjusts the amount of space between lines. We'll come to the specific ways in which the freelance writer needs to use all these controls later, in the chapter on presentation of your work. For now, let's concentrate a little more on actual typing techniques.

The best way to begin typing is to begin typing. The beginner is often tempted to start by putting everything down in long-hand, then laboriously transferring it later to the typewritten page. I've known writers who have written 80,000 word novels in this way, but if we're talking about *commercial* writing, we're talking about speed, and it's in your interests to type your words right from the start.

A piece of advice here to the non-typist, trying his or her hand at typing for the first time: do it in private. If you do it with other people around - especially other people who can type — you'll make a fool of yourself, you'll get embarrassed and you'll probably give it all up. When you first approach the keyboard, you'll be slow and clumsy. You'll search for every letter before you press the key. It will seem to take ages to write just one sentence. But, before long, if you keep at it, you'll surprise yourself about how speedy you become. I don't say that you'll be able to hit keys without looking at them, the way a touch typist does, but with your eyes down on the keyboard, you'll soon start hitting every key you need without thinking. It's amazing how fast your brain adapts, turning thoughts into words, words into letters, letters into individual key strokes on the machine.

If you want to take a proper typing course at this stage, then by all means go ahead. But you can still be a commercial writer without it. The main thing is not to be tempted to use two fingers only. I've seen professional writers get up a terrific speed by making a ball of their fists, extending one finger from each hand and attacking the keyboard with two rigid digits, bouncing off the keys like twin pogo sticks. But a far better way, I reckon, is to use as many fingers as possible. As far as a real typist is concerned, they won't be the *correct* fingers, but their use will lead to a far more comfortable way of working even so. Always use your thumb, not a finger, for the space bar, only put one space between each word, but put two spaces between sentences—it makes your copy look more professional.

Other common controls include the backspace key that takes you one space back each time you hit it, in order to make corrections; the margin release, that allows you to go beyond your set margins without resetting them; the tab cancel, that takes out the settings you have made on the tab; and the paper release, that frees the paper from the roller to be adjusted in any way you fancy.

There are many different kinds of typewriter, each performing a similar function, but in a different way. We'll look at the basic options open to you.

Manual typewriters

There are several different kinds of typewriter, each with its own advantages, disadvantages and price. The oldest kind—but one which is still very much in vogue—is the manual. This is a purely mechanical machine. Press a key and, by a series of jointed levers, an arm flies up and hits the paper through a ribbon, printing the required letter. The harder you hit the keys, the bolder the words look on paper. The ribbons are used over and over again, travelling from spool to spool through the machine and automatically reversing their direction when they get to each end. Being purely manual, the machine offers the advantage of allowing you to hit the keys harder as the ribbon gets older and more worn. Sometimes manual ribbons seem to go on forever, getting fainter and fainter all the time. If you go for this type of machine, don't let that happen. Change the ribbon when the type becomes grey not invisible. Clearly-written copy will help you sell.

There are two types of manual typewriter: good, solid office machines and much smaller portables. Of the new machines on the market, manuals are mostly confined to portables, many manufacturers of office equipment having gone over almost exclusively to electronic models. The result is that portable manuals have become almost toys. They're okay, for occasional use in the home, but they might not stand up to the day-to-day pounding that you're thinking of giving them. Also, their light weight can be an annoyance, slipping as they do about the desk as you type or push the carriage back.

If you want to make a start with a manual, then my advice is to go for a good, reconditioned, second-hand office model. There are plenty still on the market at very reasonable prices.

Electric typewriters

An electric typewriter, as opposed to an *electronic* typewriter, is very much like a manual model. On most, pressing the keys activates an arm that flies up and hits the paper by way of a ribbon. The only difference is that the action is not completely mechanical. Each key is, in effect, a switch that sets the operation in motion. Also the carriage that has to be pushed back by hand on a manual machine is returned automatically at the press of a key on the electric typewriter's keyboard. Many other functions, like margins and tabulators are purely mechanical.

A slightly different version of the electric machine is one that uses what's known as a golf-ball printing system. Here, instead of letters being on individual keys, they are all arranged around the surface of a metal ball that twists and turns to the correct position, prior to striking the ribbon. On some golf-ball machines, the carriage remains stationary, the golf-ball itself travelling along the line of type. On others, the golf-ball is static and the carriage moves between letters the way it does on purely manual machines.

Ribbons on older electric machines are the same as those found on manuals. On newer models, they might take the form of a cartridge. Either way, you'll be able to get fabric ribbons which run backwards and forwards through the machine until they are worn out, or carbon ribbons, which give a much blacker, clearer typeface, but which can be run though the machine only once. Unlike a manual, pressure on the keys does not produce a harder strike on the ribbon, but an electric will have a control to vary the striking power, allowing you to increase it as a fabric ribbon gets older.

Some electric machines offer little refinements like in-built correcting ribbons that can be used to delete characters where necessary, but by and large features like this work best on the electronic machines we'll be looking at next. When electric models first appeared on the market, they were naturally hailed as a great step forward in typewriter design, but viewed in retrospect, they appear, these days, to represent little more than a transition between the old manuals and today's ultra-sophisticated electronic models. As such, electrics in the purest sense of the word, are becoming a dying breed. Professional office machines today are of the electronic type, although there are still a lot of electric portables on the market. They are not recommended to the serious writer, suffering as they do from all the faults of a manual portable and combining these with a tendency, in some models, to overheat after a lot of serious use.

Electronic typewriters

Here, for the first time, the micro-chip makes its appearance - and what a difference it has made to typewriter design. All functions of the machine are now handled electronically. The actual printing on an electronic machine is usually by way of a daisy-wheel. This is in the form of a disc with all the characters around its outside edge. As you press a key, the disc swiftly rotates to the correct place, then stamps itself against a ribbon to print the letter onto the paper. The whole assembly moves backwards and forwards across the width of the paper, so that no moving carriage is involved. Other functions such as margins and tabulators are set electronically at the touch of a key, the machine keeping the various settings in its memory until you switch off. On some, the memory can even be retained *after* you switch the machine off, providing it is switched on again at fairly regular intervals.

Most electronic machines have memories that retain at least one line of print. Coupled with an in-built correction ribbon, this allows you to return to any point in a current line and begin deleting. More sophisticated machines have memories that can retain whole pages of copy, so that you can use them to reprint the same document over and over again, or perhaps keep certain names and addresses in the memory to head up letters. But for the average writer, an electronic machine with enough memory to deal with the correction facilities is perfectly adequate.

Most electronic machines work on carbon ribbons that give very clear lettering, but which can only be used once. Daisy wheels are interchangeable to give different typefaces for different uses.

Word processors

A word processor represents the most sophisticated method yet of handling copy. When you first hear about them, it's easy to think that they're too complicated and that they actually do *too* much. Nothing could be further from the truth. Once you've read the instruction book a word processor is as easy to operate as an electronic typewriter, and it will offer untold advantages to a writer who demands good-quality copy with speed.

The system is based on a small computer. In some instances, the word processing facilities are part of a typical business computer; in others, you can have a normal home computer adapted with software or with an extra chip that plugs straight into the computer's ROM. Either way, you don't have to be a computer expert to operate one.

When you type copy into a word processor, it does not appear straight away on paper in the way it would with a typewriter. Instead, it appears on a VDU screen. You set margins and tabulators just the same as you would on an electronic typewriter, then cover the screen in print. When you have finished writing, you check it over and make your corrections—which is where the word processor really comes into its own. Now you can insert or delete letters, complete words or whole lines. You can move quickly from the top of your copy to the bottom, search for particular words, change words throughout with a single command, split lines up, join others together, reformat the whole page to a different margin width, justify the copy (straight margin at left *and* right of the page), delete blocks of text, move other blocks from one place to another, automatically centre certain lines, program certain words to appear at the top and bottom of every page, initiate a system to automatically number each page consecutively, count the words you've written as you go along . . .

What it comes down to is this. You can make all the changes electronically that you might normally make with a pencil after you've written your first draft. What's more you can see those changes presented on the screen before you instantly. Finally, and only when you are completely satisfied with the way your copy looks on the screen, you print the whole thing out on paper.

That's done with a printer, which is like an electronic typewriter without a keyboard. Alternatively, some models of electronic typewriter double as printers. Whichever way you work, the word processor finally prints out a copy of the work you have been writing in exactly the way you want it. The words can be printed on individual sheets of paper, or they can be printed on continuous stationery—sheets of A4-sized paper, folded concertina fashion and perforated at each fold. Once printed, the individual sheets can easily be separated and clipped together like ordinary single sheets of paper.

At any time along the way, you can store the words you have written on disc. This is achieved by a simple command from the keyboard of the word processor and is almost instantaneous. It takes no more than a few seconds to store, say, 1,000 words of copy and just another few seconds to call those words up again for later use.

I have no hesitation in saying that a word processor has changed the way I write. Before investing in one, my system looked like this: type first draft, correct it, retype it as accurately as possible with a carbon, then make final corrections. These days, with a word processor, the first draft is the final draft because everything is corrected electronically before commitment to paper, and there's no need for a carbon because everything is kept on disc until no longer required. After that, the disc is wiped for use again.

If you have a lot of work, a word processor can actually double your output—and deliver neater, more accurate copy into the bargain.

Tape recorders

There are two types of tape recorder that are useful to the writer: straightforward recording machines, either in the normal form that takes a standard cassette or in a smaller version that takes a micro cassette, and dictating machines. Don't get the two mixed up.

If you are doing a lot of interviews and you don't want to trust the old notebook and pencil way, then by all means use a small tape recorder. But make sure it actually is a recorder, such as the type found in the Olympus Pearlcorder range, for instance, and not merely the dictating part of a dictating machine. They look similar, but they work in different ways. A true recorder will work some distance from your subject, so that you can lay it on a table between you and forget about it. The dictating handset is designed to only really work at its best when used close.

So if it's interviews you're after, go for a straight tape recorder. On the other hand, if you feel that you can actually dictate your writing, rather than putting it all on paper, then by all means invest in a dictating machine. You can carry the small recorder part with you at all times, dictating your copy at any time you like; the tape then fits into a playback machine that a typist can use to transcribe your words onto paper.

Pens and paper

Finally, don't skimp on the small details like pens and paper. Remember that first impressions count for a lot in this business and neatness of presentation can say a lot for your work. Use pens that will give a bold but fairly thin stroke, making it easy to add final corrections to your work where necessary without any confusion over your writing. Stick to normal colours like black or blue, working with ball-point or fine felt-tip pens.

There are two types of paper that will be useful to you. You'll need good-quality for your top copies, but if you are taking carbons, you can go for something lighter for your own files. The type of paper usually used for top copies is called Bond and the thinner paper, used for carbons, is called Bank. Stick to white and standardise on A4—the most common paper size used by writers for the type of work we're dealing with here.

Other bits and pieces that will come in useful include a good heavy-duty office stapling machine, bottles of correcting fluid, plenty of paper clips and a good dictionary.

Put it all together and you'll have what it takes to start writing. All you need now is to find out what to write and where to sell it. Which is where we're moving to next.

THE MAGAZINE MARKET

"Everyone lives by selling something."
—Robert Louis Stevenson

If you want to start making money from what you write, you must begin by producing a saleable commodity. What you write must be needed by someone. You have to give the market what it wants, not what you think it ought to have.

Think of yourself as a kind of literary greengrocer. A greengrocer sells fruit and vegetables, you sell words on paper. A greengrocer won't sell exotic fruits to the customer who has only a need for a couple of pounds of potatoes for the Sunday lunch, just as you won't sell highly-artistic prose to the market that needs a more down-to-earth article. The greengrocer won't sell bad fruit and you won't sell bad writing. Anyone in business will tell you that the way to *stay* in business is to give the customers what they want—and it's no different in the world of commercial writing. The trick is to first find out what's needed and then to supply those needs exactly.

So where do you start? Probably the very best place is in your local newsagent, browsing along the racks of magazines. The magazine market is vast. Around 7,000 different titles are published in the UK alone and every one is full of words—a great many of which you could be in a position to supply. Magazines are undoubtedly the biggest and most lucrative market for the freelance writer.

Types of magazine

You must first recognise that despite the fact that there are thousands of different magazines on the market, and despite the fact that there might be as many as twenty at a time dealing with the same basic subject, each magazine is different. Each has its own slot in the marketplace. Even when two or more magazines are dealing with the same subject, they will be handling it in different ways.

Take car magazines, for instance. At first sight, they might all look alike. But dig deeper and you'll see that one magazine might deal only with modern cars, while another concentrates on vintage and collectors' cars; one is about normal everyday cars, another exclusively about sports cars; one magazine deals with driving the cars, another looks only at repairing them; one magazine might be aimed at the car buyer, another at the people who sell them. And it's the same with every other market. Computers? There are magazines aimed exclusively at specific makes, plus others for hobbyists, businessmen or those who want only to play games. Boats? Are we talking about yachts at sea, or narrow boats on canals, weekend sailors or those interested only in racing? Cameras? Are your readers interested in actual pictures or only the equipment that takes them, are they pure beginners, advanced amateurs or even professionals?

Every magazine has its market and, before you even attempt to sell to it, you need to know what that market is. So you start by making a market analysis.

Analysing your market

Write about what you know. That's one of the pieces of advice you'll always hear handed out to aspiring writers, and while I don't say it's the be all and end all of freelance writing, I'd definitely agree that it's a good way to start. Everyone knows something about something, so start from there. Pick a subject and then look at your options.

Are you going to write about that subject for the consumer or for the trade? There are magazines for each. A consumer magazine is aimed at the person who has a general interest in your subject and maybe wants to learn a little more about the subject itself. A trade magazine is aimed more at the marketing of the product and will be read by the people who make their living from your chosen subject. Consumer magazines will be readily available in newsagents, whereas trade magazines might be harder to find, since many of them are sold on subscription straight to the people who need them. If you want to find out more about trade magazines, speak to people who are in the appropriate business. You'll also find a list of the major titles in a publication called *The Freelance Photographer's Market Handbook*, published annually by BFP Books. It's aimed at freelance photographers, but it's full of useful information for freelance writers too and so is worth getting hold of.

Having made that distinction between consumer and trade magazines, it must be said that the aspiring freelance will probably aim first at the consumer press.

So, having decided on your subject, begin to look at the magazines involved with that subject. Learn to see how they handle it, who they aim themselves at and the level of expertise that's assumed in the readers. Just looking at these simple basics will bring you down to perhaps a couple of different titles and finally to the one at which you are going to aim your work. Now you're ready to begin your analysis in earnest.

Discovering a magazine's needs

Your first stop is on the contents page. There, apart from the list of feature articles to be found in that issue, you'll also find details of the magazine's in-house staff. Look to see how many there are on the editorial side. You're looking for titles like editor, assistant editor, features editor, technical editor, reporters, staff writers—not that many magazines will have such a full complement. It's far more likely that the total editorial staff comprises no more than an editor and an assistant. It stands to reason, of course, that the less staff actually involved in the production of the magazine in-house, the more they're going to need freelances like yourself, so it is in your best interest to pick a magazine with a small staff. There will be other staff listed on this page, but many of these can be ignored, simply because they are not involved in actually writing the magazine and so pose no great threat to the work you are out to place. Among these, you can count the likes of publishers, editorial directors, production editors, layout and design workers and advertisement staff.

Having sorted out in your mind which names are concerned with production of words in the magazine, you can now look through the pages, or maybe simply run your eyes down the contents list, to see how the names on the list match up to the bylines on the features. (A *byline*, by the way, is the printed name of the person who wrote the article.) The features that are always handled by the in-house staff are the ones you ignore, because there is obviously no place here for a freelance. Next look for the regular contributors. The best way of discovering who these are is to look at more than one copy of the magazine. If names not on the staff list appear regularly in every issue, it's a good bet they belong to regular contributors, and once again the sort of work they are regularly supplying is outside your reach at the moment. There is no reason why you shouldn't become a regular yourself in time, if you can supply the magazine with its needs, but right at the start, you should steer clear of invading the regulars' territory.

Now that you know what's *not* available to you, you can begin looking for what *is*. Don't be discouraged by the fact that we've found a lot of places where you won't sell because, when you come to look closely, you might find that the magazine's staff handle only things like news pages, reviews of equipment and perhaps one other feature in each issue; regular contributors might also be involved in equipment testing, but more than likely, they'll be supplying personally-written features on specialised subjects. When you come to look closely at the magazine, you could easily find a lot more areas that are open to the general freelance - and that's where you come in.

Style and content

By now, you'll obviously know the principal subject covered by your chosen magazine, and your next task is to find out what sort of *approach* they take to that subject. Read the various features very carefully and ask yourself questions like these . . .

Are the features aimed at men or women? Few magazines on today's market cater for both sexes. In some cases, the differences are obvious: *Woman's Own* and the like are obviously aimed at women; *Men Only* is primarily aimed at men. But even magazines without such obvious guidelines in the title are usually produced for one or the other. Craft magazines might be aimed at a female readership, while the majority of hobby magazines, dealing with everything from model railways to motorbikes, assume their readership to be male.

What age group reads the magazines? Again, some titles are obvious. Magazines concerned with the pop industry will be aimed at the young, those that deal with pensions and what to do when you retire are for the older person. But age plays its part too in other, less obvious titles. Certain hobbies are practised more at one age than at another, and so that's where the magazine's style and content will be aimed. Decide from the subject and the magazine's approach who is reading the magazine and it will tell you a lot about how to write for it.

What class of person is catered for? Like it or not, this country is divided into classes, from working class through to upper class. Different classes have different interests and the magazines they read will reflect these. Looking at the advertisements can often help you here. A magazine that is full of advertisements for expensive, up-market property isn't going to be interested in a feature about how to cut costs by servicing your own car.

Are the features aimed at beginners or experts? Many magazines deal with hobbies and there are always different levels of hobbyists. Some are just starting out, others know the basics but want to learn a little more, some want really advanced techniques explained. Look at your magazine to see which is the case. You won't sell by aiming elementary knowledge at the expert or by being too clever for the beginner.

How personalised are the features? Are they written in a straight, informative way from the third person viewpoint, or do they take a more informal approach, talking about the subject in the first person, from the personal experience of the writer, maybe even throwing in a little anecdote here and there? If your chosen magazine likes its features straight, you should not attempt to introduce a personal note to your writing.

What about the grammatical style? Some magazines go for pure English without any deviation from what is considered to be correct grammar. Others have a more trendy approach to writing, using slang words and a more down-market style. Whichever is the case, you should stick to what they want.

How do they feel about opinion? Some magazines like the facts straight, others are happy to allow the writer a personal opinion on his or her subject. Don't introduce opinion where it's not needed if you want to succeed in selling.

How serious is the writing? In some markets, it's deadly serious, others are willing to allow a certain amount of whimsy to creep in. If the straight and narrow is what they want, don't give them anything else.

How common is their subject matter? Does the magazine cover a subject that is well-known to everyone, or is it more concerned with an unusual, slightly off-beat subject? Don't give the obvious to a market that wants something more out of the ordinary.

Asking yourself questions like these is going to give you a whole new way of looking at magazines. You're no longer looking at them in the way the reader does when he or she reads an article to learn certain facts. Instead, you're looking *beneath* the facts and *between* the lines to see just what this magazine wants and how it uses the words on its pages. Basic questions like those above—and probably more that you'll think of for yourself once you get the knack—will give you an idea of the style you need to adopt for your market, but equally important is the *length* of the article. The place where so many aspiring writers go wrong is in the length of what they write. Either they write too much or they write too little—usually the latter, because they don't research their subject enough and soon run out of things to say.

Ways around that particular problem will be dealt with in the next chapter—meanwhile sort out in your mind what sort of length of article your market needs. Do that by counting words. You don't have to count each one individually because there is an easy way to make a pretty accurate estimate. First measure an inch down one column and count the number of words in that inch. Then measure the total number of column inches in the feature and multiply one figure by the other. The estimated figure this gives you is perfectly close enough to guide you towards their needs.

Although we are talking essentially about writing here, it is also worth assessing the photographic needs of the magazine. Do they use features that consist only of words? If there is a picture with the feature, is it the type that is there only for dressing and which might have come from the magazine's files? Or are the features all picture-oriented? If the latter is the case, you might find your chances bettered if you can supply some pictures with your words—either your own or from a working partnership with a photographer. We'll come back to that line of thought a little later.

Let's take a look now at some of the more popular types of magazines on the market and how making the sort of analysis we've been talking about can lead you to a better understanding of the requirements of each.

County magazines

Most counties in the British Isles have their own magazines, each one dealing with interesting people, facts and events concerning the locality. They make a good starting point for the freelance writer.

Because they are often run on a shoestring, the in-house staff of such magazines is usually quite small and they rely a geat deal on freelances. You'll find them interested in articles on subjects such as local history, interesting villages or towns, local people who have a strange or unusual hobby, other people who are in the news for various reasons—in fact anything and everything that is local to the particular county covered by the magazine.

The thing to beware of with this market is the temptation to be too obvious. Certain counties contain famous villages that everyone in the county has heard about, usually because of their historical associations or maybe because they are particularly beautiful. While this is the type of subject that a county magazine might favour in theory, the practice is that they will already have covered such a well-known local landmark many times before. Also, the fact that most people in the county also know about the place would mean that your feature might not generate as much interest as you at first thought. The answer is to be less obvious in your approach. Find a really out-of-the-way village that's worth talking about; if you must go for well-known places, try to dig out some unusual or little-known facts that will be of interest to the readers; find some interesting personalities who have something unusual to say. Remember that you will never sell by telling readers everything they already know; tell them something that surprises, educates or entertains them and you'll always increase your chances of success.

Hobby magazines

Here is an enormous sector of the magazine market. There are magazines for just about every hobby you can think of, and very often there are several different magazines all covering the same hobby. In those circumstances, you must first look at the market the way we've already dealt with above—trying to find out exactly at whom the magazine is aimed and the level of the reader's competence.

Go for a prestigious hobby like photography and you'll find magazines with quite a big staffing level, much of the work being done in-house. But go for a lesser hobby, such as model building, and you'll find the magazines have a much smaller staff, some even being put together by no more than an editor without so much as an assistant. Such magazines obviously rely fairly heavily on freelances.

When you write for a hobby magazine, you must never lose sight of who your reader is. He or she is someone who knows a good bit about the subject you are covering, but who wants to know more. Just as with so many other branches of this business, it doesn't pay to be obvious. Don't tell the reader what he or she already knows. Find new angles, dig that little deeper to find new facts, enlarge your reader's knowledge and you'll win every time.

General interest magazines

Contrary to popular belief, there are very few genuine general interest magazines in today's market. It is far more usual for magazines to be aimed at a very particular specialist interest. Nevertheless, there are a few around which are designed to be read by anyone and everyone who just wants a modicum of fast entertainment for a few minutes.

Mostly these magazines deal with slightly off-beat subjects: little-known facts, strange tales from different parts of the world, unusual historical stories and the like. They are often interested in show-business features and they have a liking for short, sharp humorous pieces. They usually feature a pretty lively letters page too, with payment for each letter published. Get the style of the letter they like right and even this can give you a steady little income.

Holiday and travel magazines

Again, there are not as many actual magazines dealing with travel as the freelance often thinks. There are a few, but more often this type of subject will be better catered for in other types of magazine. Certain women's magazines, for instance, will run holiday specials at the right time of the year, while specialist interest magazines such as those dealing with camping or caravanning will provide a place for words about various parts of the UK or the world in general—providing, of course, you get your angles right. If you're writing for a caravanning magazine, make sure you're dealing with an area that is accessible to caravans.

Other than these markets, others that actually want words about holiday locations will usually be looking for the unusual and the different. In other words, the delights of the Canadian Rockies in Spring will go down a lot better than a description of your fun-filled fortnight in Spain. As with everything else in this game, it all comes down to telling your readers about something which is genuinely interesting or entertaining, rather than something which is obvious.

Women's magazines

Here is another sector of the market about which a complete book could be written. This country has a frankly enormous volume of women's magazines, all aimed at different types, ages and classes of reader. You have only to look at a woman's magazine to see the fundamental difference between male and female readers. While men read a magazine that is aimed at a hobby, pastime or specialist interest, women read magazines that, in general, encompass the whole world of feminine interests from babies to fashion, from make-up to cookery.

With so many different women's magazines being published, it's pretty well true to say that you can find a market among them for almost any subject under the sun. Essentially, of course, the subjects must be of interest to women, but these by no means stop at the traditional topics mentioned above. These days women are interested in everything from car maintenance to hang-gliding, and many of the more liberated magazines will publish articles on subjects that, just a few years back, would have seemed a long way outside their domain. It's all a matter of studying your market. While certain magazines do go for this wide approach, it's equally true to say that there are others which still keep to a more traditional style of publication, full of cake making and knitting patterns.

One problem with women's magazines, as far as the freelance is concerned, lies in the fact that they have such big staff levels. It's not unusual for a magazine to have editors with assistants and even secretaries and writers for each of the big subjects like cookery, fashion and beauty. So, when you come to thinking up ideas for this market, try to steer clear of the staff writers' territory.

Never try to sell to a woman's magazine without first making a detailed analysis in the ways we dealt with earlier in this chapter. With so many different publications in the marketplace, they really do all need to be just that little bit different from even their nearest rivals if they are going to stay in business. Only by analysing your market carefully will you spot that difference and see where best to sell your ideas.

House magazines

One market that is often ignored by the freelance writer is that of the house magazine. You won't see these on sale at your local newsagent; in fact you'll be lucky to see them for sale anywhere. Mostly they are free and given away to the employees of large companies. But they can still provide an income for the freelance.

Many large companies have house magazines. They deal obviously with subjects connected with the company concerned—news about its products, features about its employees—but they can offer quite a range of possibilities. Say you have been interviewing a man about an unusual hobby for a county magazine. If you find he works in a large company that is likely to have its own house magazine, then ask your subject about it. There's every chance that he will have a copy of the magazine for you to look at. Sending them your feature, written with a slightly different angle to that of the county magazine, might easily give you two sales for the price of one.

When you are a freelance, you need to be continually on the look-out for different markets and it's wise to remember that the most obvious one—the magazine that you see prominently displayed on the bookstalls — isn't the *only* one. Neither is it always the most lucrative. House magazines won't put your name up in lights, but they are usually funded by the company's public relations budget and, when it comes to paying, they often hand out higher fees than even top-selling consumer magazines.

RESEARCHING FOR MAGAZINES

"Now what I want is Facts . . . Facts alone are wanted in life."
—Charles Dickens

The words you read above come from the fictional mouth of Mr. Gradgrind in *Hard Times*. He wasn't talking about the art of researching for magazines, but he might as well have been. Because facts are the foundation on which you build features. Without them, there would be no basis for a magazine article in the first place; without them, the writer would have nothing to write about and the reader would have nothing worthwhile to read.

But before you get round to gathering your facts, you first need an idea for a feature—the subject around which you are going to build your article. It's not difficult to find subject matter of all types, once you get the knack. It's what newspaper reporters call having a nose for a good story.

Finding ideas

In the last chapter, we looked at ways of finding the right magazine for your needs and how to analyse it to discover the requirements. Now we're going one step further and looking at actual subjects for articles. There are subjects all around you—which is easy for someone already experienced in the business to say. For the newcomer, it's not always as easy to understand. What you must do, then, is to look at the world with different eyes, the way you've already learnt to look differently at magazines.

Perhaps one of the most important things to remember is not to be too obvious. It's all too easy to discover some interesting fact or set of facts for yourself and think they will interest the readers of a magazine when, in fact, those facts are already well-known to most.

So look for subjects which are just a little different or out of the ordinary. Look for interesting stories of your locality. A little research into the history of certain local landmarks might give you what you're looking for. Look for people with interesting occupations or hobbies. The local newspaper is a good source of information here. Look in the classified advertisements, in the *Articles Wanted* columns to see what people are advertising for. Unusual objects often mean unusual hobbies, and they can make stories. While you're at it, look through the news and features in the actual news pages. Local newspaper reporters are extremely parochial. They'll often see a good local story, but never think it's worth writing up for a national magazine. With the training you are beginning to get for yourself, you'll see a greater potential to stories right on your own doorstep. Look for local personalities with unusual views on certain subjects. They too can provide the ideas on which you might be able to build an entire article.

Go back to your hobbies and the hobbies of your friends and acquaintances. Perhaps you know someone who is interested in stripping down and rebuilding vintage cars. Work with him to see how he goes about it, step-by-step to make an article for the specialist motoring press. How about someone else who is keen on do-it-yourself and has discovered some interesting short cuts to getting common jobs around the house done? Get his tips down on paper and you could have an article. How about a girl or woman who has a job or hobby more usually associated with a man? Sounds like the start of a feature for a woman's magazine.   Look about you both at home and when you go on holiday. You might come across an organisation, a business or a club that does unusual work of some kind. Find the man or woman who runs things and you'll have the basis for a magazine article.

Look back at your own personal experiences. The problems you might have had in buying and selling a house, all the funny things that went wrong with the car you bought, an unusual job you might have had at one time and the strange characters you might have met. Things like this can often make the basis for personal experience pieces.

Or how about a strong opinion you might hold on certain topics? The way manufacturers badly-write instructions, for instance, or perhaps the way the English language gets tortured by certain people or publications. If you have a hobby horse, get on it and ride it. Strongly, cleverly and amusingly written words on all sorts of different topics work well as short articles for certain types of magazine.

I used to work on a provincial newspaper, on which we had a demon reporter called Bill. Bill continually turned in the best stories and features— really top-notch news stories, and features about people with weird or unusual hobbies and occupations. He was the best reporter on the paper, and seemed to be able to dig out subjects for his stories and features that left everyone else in the office standing. One day, I asked him how he did it.

"Simple," he replied. "I get up in the morning, wash, shave and have breakfast. I get dressed and I go out the front door. I walk down the road and the first person I see, I stop and, very politely, I say, 'Excuse me, I'm from the local newspaper, do you have any news today?' Much of the time, the person says no, or tells me to clear off, so I pass on and stop the next person I see. I rarely get beyond six people before I have a story."

To this day, I don't know whether I fully believed him or not, but the fact is that the basic premise was extremely sound. Everyone has a story in them, once you get the knack of coaxing it out of them—or if you have the courage to stop complete strangers in the street and talk to them the way Bill reckoned he did. Just talking to people and listening to them will very often give you a story or the basis for a magazine article. The fact is that people in general have all got stories to tell, but only *you* are trained in seeing the commercial potential in what they have to say.

How often have you heard someone say something like: "A funny thing happened to a mate of mine the other day . . ."

Or: "I met a bloke last week who keeps a baby alligator in his bath . . ."

Or: "My mate George has got it cracked. You'll never believe what he does for a living . . ."

Or: "I discovered a very strange thing about the road we live in the other day . . ."

Talk to people. Listen to what they have to say and you'll be amazed what can come out at times.

Most of all, look at the magazines themselves. Especially, of course, look at the specific magazine that you have chosen as your target. Look to see what sort of subjects they continually publish and how they handle them.

Then look round to see where you can find similar subjects.

To the beginner, finding a subject for your proposed article can seem to be an impossibility at the start. But once you begin to develop a nose for a story, you'll soon find that there are subjects all around you. And remember, it's not always *where* you look that counts, it's *how*.

Conducting an interview

Before you begin to write your feature, you have to gather your facts. There are several ways you can do this, but perhaps one of the most common is by interviewing someone on their subject. It's not difficult to arrange an interview. All you have to do is contact the person who has the facts that you need, introduce yourself, tell the person that you are a freelance writer and that you think that his or her knowledge can help you put a feature together, and arrange a time and place to meet. You'll find that the majority of people are delighted to help. There is something flattering about being asked questions on a topic that you know something about and, for many interviewees, the whole thing is a bit of an ego trip. So don't be nervous about making the contact. Few people, you'll find, will turn you down.

The actual interview, on the other hand, is a different matter. The first time you try your hand at it, you'll probably be a little nervous. That's natural, but really there is nothing to be nervous about, and if you prepare yourself well in advance, you should find things running smoothly.

Before the interview, think carefully about what sort of facts you need to gather, what sort of questions you need answered. Make a list of questions that you feel are important. When you come to conduct the interview, don't be afraid of referring to this list. Equally, don't be afraid to deviate from it, as one question naturally leads to another. But if the time comes when you run out of things to ask, then you can always return to your list.

The questions to ask

When you come to prepare your questions, there are six key words that will prompt you to get the main facts. The words are these: *Who, What, How, Where, When* and *Why*. Keep those six words in your mind and make sure you ask at least one question connected with one of those words. More importantly, make sure you get a satisfactory answer. Here's an example of how those key words might translate into the right sort of questions. Let's say, for instance, that you are interviewing a bee-keeper about his hobby.

Who are you? This introduces the reader to the subject of the feature. Here we learn who the person is and what sort of a person he or she is. If the subject is a woman, knowing how many children she has is often relevant, as well as her age. (*Twenty-eight-year old mother of two Betty Smith has a rather unusual hobby. She keeps bees . . .*) Age is also important if it is unusual as far as the subject of the feature is concerned. It might not be too unusual for a man in his forties or fifties to keep bees, but a twelve-year-old schoolboy, a ninety-one year old pensioner, or a nineteen-year-old beauty queen are different matters entirely.

What do you do? Here we get the basics of what the feature is all about. He or she keeps bees.

How do you do it? Now we get down to the explanations. This is where the reader learns the art of bee-keeping and how the subject carries out his or her hobby. This is the place to explain everything in simple terms and look out for any unusual angles that might present themselves.

Where do you do it? This is a question that can be more relevant at certain times than at others. If our hero is keeping bees in a field outside a big country house, then there's nothing much to say. But suppose they are being kept in the tiny back garden of a council house? Or on the roof of a block of flats? Suddenly there's a new angle and a better story.

When do you do it? Again, the answer is more relevant at one time than at another. If the answer is a traditional one, fine; if it's not, you've got another angle.

Why do you do it? This is the question that can give you a real insight into your subject's character. His or her reaction to this question can open up completely new angles. Why does he or she keep bees? Because it's a family tradition. Because she was fed up with the price of honey in the local supermarket and decided to make her own. Because he has started a local business selling honey. Because they just like bees . . . So many different answers with so many different angles for your feature.

Obviously, talking this way about one particular subject like bee-keeping restricts the way these examples of typical answers might turn out. With other subjects, certain questions—and their answers—will be more important than others. But these are the basics that will lead you towards thinking of other questions that will help you get all the facts you need to know.

Conducting the actual interview, once you have your list of questions, is an art that is soon learnt. First off, if you feel nervous, try not to show it. Go into the interview calmly and confidently. Remember that very often the interviewee might be even more nervous. It's your job to put him or her at ease.

Don't launch straight into your questions the moment you are through the door. Instead, start with a little small talk, then gradually ease yourself into the interview. If you aim to use a tape recorder, always ask the subject's permission. Few object these days, but one or two might. I have always found that the best way to conduct an interview is with a tape recorder, but using a notebook at the same time. This serves a number of purposes. It gives you somewhere to write down difficult spellings of unusual specialist words—including the subject's name very often, it provides a natural place to keep your list of questions without making it too obvious to your subject and it gives you a place to stop and write when you run out of things to say, allowing you to gather your thoughts and work out what your next question might be.

When you ask your questions, be direct. Don't mumble or ask ambiguous questions that are difficult to understand, let alone answer. Don't ask negative questions. That means you should never say something like: "I don't suppose you could tell me why you started keeping bees." Instead, you should say something more like: "Why did you start keeping bees?"

Always allow your subject time to answer. Once they have started, don't interrupt. Let them have their say. When they have finished, don't be too quick to leap straight in with your next question, but instead, allow a small pause. Very often, the subject will think of something to add and carry on with a new line of thought that's even more interesting.

Allow one question to lead naturally to the next. Don't change the subject with every question you ask. If the answer involves something you don't understand, don't be afraid to ask for clarification. After all it's the person in front of you who is the expert, not you. If you knew as much as he or she did, then you wouldn't be conducting the interview in the first place. So always let the answer dictate your next question, but when you have exhausted all the angles on that question, then revert to your list.

Don't let your subject waffle. If he or she begins to drift right off the subject, guide them firmly and politely back on course.

Never let an interview go on too long. Most people will enjoy talking about themselves for an hour or so, but after that the interview can begin to get boring for both sides. When this begins to happen, it's time to wrap things up.

Finish by having a quick glance through your list to make certain you've forgotten nothing, then double-check with your six key words. At the end of the interview, make sure you have the subject's name correctly written down and ask for a telephone number so that you can check any final details later. When you first start interviewing, you'll always forget one or two important questions, and it won't be until you begin to write the feature that you'll remember what you forgot!

Be courteous throughout, thank your subject for his or her time and don't take up any more of it than is necessary. Leave them with the feeling that you have each had a pleasant chat and you won't have any difficulties coming back for more details later, should you require them.

Research from books

There's an old saying that goes like this: Copying from one book is plagiarism; copying from two books is research. What it means it that there is no way that you can take something written in a book and present it as your own work for a magazine. But what you can take from several books are *facts*. Facts are facts. There is no copyright on them. But care is needed in the way you take them from one source and present them to another. Let's say, for instance, that you have decided to write an article on something like the history of London. There must have been hundreds of books written on the subject, but that doesn't detract from the fact that a magazine might well be interested in a piece on one particular aspect of the city's history.

Taking the necessary facts from one book only could present problems later. If the author saw your article and recognised the fact that you have used *only* the information that he used in his book, then he would have fair grounds for complaint. Use two or three books for your research, making certain that all your facts don't necessarily come from the same source, and you can rightly say that you have not stolen anyone else's work. There's another advantage in using more than one book for your research: it gives you a chance to double-check the known facts against different sources. Just because facts are presented in a book, don't think that makes them sacrosanct. Authors make mistakes just like everyone else and it's all too easy to end up taking inaccurate facts and presenting them as the truth. So double check the same facts against as many different sources from as many different books by different authors as you can get hold of. That way you'll stand a good chance of getting things right most of the time. Also, if any one of those authors ever did accuse you of stealing their ideas, you can easily point out all the others who appear to have done exactly the same thing in all the other books with which you have been working.

Where do you find books from which to research? The best place is obviously in the reference section of your local library. A few hours there, looking through books on a wide range of topics can give you enough ideas for a whole lot of different magazine features. What sort of books? Encyclopedias, history books, geography books, books on unusual or weird phenomena, to name just a few. Once you start looking, you'll be amazed at just how much potential your local library can provide.

Press and public relations offices

Another place that can yield facts for your research is the press or public relations office of a large company or organisation. If, for instance, you are researching facts for a technical article on a subject such as photography or cars, you can approach the makers or importers of specific models for information. The same goes for large organisations that could range from museums or concert halls to corporations like British Telecom or the BBC. Even Buckingham Palace has a press office!

The whole point of such offices is to obtain maximum publicity for a certain product, so if you can show the press officer or public relations head that you are in a position to get publicity for the product, then you will have no difficulty in obtaining information.

Many press or public relations departments have ready-made information in the form of leaflets, fact sheets or press packs on specific products, and all of these will be available free, providing you can show them that you are making genuine inquiries about their product and that you are in a position to get them publicity.

Naturally, the information you get from these offices will talk in terms of their individual products as the best on the market. The information won't (or *shouldn't*) be innaccurate, but it will be biased. It's therefore up to you to sort out the facts from the boasts. One way is to get information on the same type of product from several different, rival companies, then compare and extract the actual facts from each company's literature.

If the organisation you are dealing with is English, then you can approach them direct. If it is a foreign import such as a Japanese camera or perhaps a German car, then you must deal with the importers. If we are talking about a small product, then it will probably be imported by an independent company; if the product is world-famous, then the importer could be an English-based subsidiary of the parent company. As an example, in the photographic world, small accessories such as those made by a Japanese company called Itorex are imported by an independent company called Dorkstar Limited, whereas major camera brands like Nikon and Canon are imported by Nikon UK Limited and Canon UK Limited.

The addresses of the manufacturers or importers can usually be found on their sales literature or, if you know the area from which they operate, in the appropriate telephone books. The best line of approach is by telephone, asking for the press officer or the department that handles public relations. Once you are put through, keep in mind that you are now connected to a very busy department. Be brief, be professional and come straight to the point, explaining who you are, what you are doing and what you need. If they have the sort of information you require, give them your address and a daytime telephone number at which they can contact you. Always ask for the name of the person to whom you are talking, so that if you need any more information at a later date, you can get straight back to the right person. It will also give you a point of contact should you not hear from them as arranged.

Contacting showbusiness personalities

One of the most popular and, for the freelance, more pleasurable magazine features to write is the one that revolves around a certain showbusiness personality. If you want to try your hand at this, there are a few ground rules. First and foremost, remember what you are in business for. You are contacting a certain personality with a view to writing a magazine article, *not* merely because you have always wanted to meet that particular person. Of course, if you can find a good reason to interview someone you really do want to meet, then so much the better. But keep in mind that business comes first.

Remember too that the person you are about to interview has been interviewed many times before, and probably by interviewers a lot more professional than you are. These are busy people who do not tolerate fools lightly, so you must go into the interview well prepared, with plenty of confidence, and be ready to get straight down to business.

In order to sell the interview, you will usually need a topical angle of some sort—the fact that the actor or actress has just landed a major TV or film role, he or she is involved in a popular soap opera, or at the very least they are appearing regularly on TV. If they have something unusual going for them—a hobby or pastime that you wouldn't naturally associate with them—then that too can give you an angle.

So you know who you want to interview and you have a reason for doing so. How do you get to meet them? What you don't do is approach them at their home address, even if you know it. You'll often see advertisments among the small ads and classified columns for lists of stars' addresses. Even if the said addresses are accurate, don't be tempted to buy the book and start making contact. The professional way to approach a showbusiness personality is through his or her agent. Their names, addresses and telephone numbers are listed in a showbusiness publication called *Spotlight*, but failing that, you can usually get the name of the appropriate agent from the press office of any film or TV company with whom the star is associated.

This is the approach that I have always used in the past, usually getting the agent's name from the press office of BBC Radio or TV, or the press office of the appropriate ITV company. A polite letter to the personality concerned, addressed to him or her, but care of the agent, will usually yield results. Say who you are, why you want to conduct the interview, enclose a stamped addressed envelope for a reply and give a daytime telephone number too. If the person concerned is agreeable to an interview, he or she will then contact you personally, either by letter or telephone, and you can arrange a meeting at a time or place that is mutually agreeable. Taking this line of approach, I have ended up interviewing a number of TV personalities, in their home, at a restaurant where I footed the bill and even in the BBC Club where the person I was interviewing treated me to lunch.

Personal experience

There is yet another type of magazine article open to the freelance writer and one that calls for no research at all, other than the examination of your own mind. This is the personal experience article. What sort of experiences are we talking about? Try unusual, weird, lucky, unlucky, traumatic, funny . . . if it happened to you and it doesn't regularly happen to other people, then it's a good bet that it will make the basis for a personal experience piece. In this area, I've sold features on my experiences with a crooked car salesman, the trouble I had getting rid of rubbish when the dustmen went on strike, the problems that arose when I found a lost horse in a country lane at midnight, the complications of selling my house and much more besides.

There's also the personal experience type of article that involves talking about your own personal reaction to certain ideas. Your reaction to the daily problems of life, what you think of the TV soap operas, why you can't stand snobs . . . find something original, unusual or controversial to say and you might find a market for your views.

All you need for this type of article is a start, a subject that sparks off ideas and the way you react to them. You don't even have to tell the truth! You might, for instance, be writing about a bad day in your life when everything went wrong. In order to make a sale, you have to ensure that the things that you are describing are feasible as well as entertaining or funny and as such, it is a good idea if they are based on things that actually did happen. But they needn't all have happened to you, they don't have to have happened all on the same day or in the order in which you describe them. And they needn't have been quite as dramatic. In this context, there is nothing wrong with a little exaggeration—providing you don't take it too far. Keep to the sort of thing that *could* have happened, rather than the sort of thing that would *never* have happened.

"Write about what you know" is one of the oldest maxims in freelance writing. It's not one to which I completely subscribe, because I think research into subjects that you don't know too much about in order to write an article can broaden your mind and give you a lot of pleasure. But at the start, your own knowledge can provide a fund of projects for different magazine features, once you get the idea of what's needed.

WRITING A MAGAZINE ARTICLE

"Let's have some new clichés."
—Samuel Goldwyn

Now we come to the nitty-gritty. You've chosen your market and done your research. Now you have the task of actually putting everything down on paper, turning the information you have gathered into a readable and interesting magazine feature. The steps you need to take are the same whatever type of feature you are preparing, whether from an interview, research or personal experience.

Your first step is to decide what you have to say and the order in which you are going to say it. With that in mind, it's best to start by making a list of the salient points of your feature. It doesn't have to be a definitive list and it doesn't even have to be intelligible to anyone but you, but it should outline the important factors that go to make up your story. Having made the list, you can then move on to putting the relevant points into some sort of order.

Putting on the style

Magazine articles and features fall into different styles and this is where you decide which style yours is going to follow. Begin by looking at your list of points and deciding how they need to be grouped, how various facts will lead naturally into each other. The facts do not have to be presented in the order in which you asked the questions at an interview or, indeed, the order in which your subject answered. Your purpose is to make a good, readable feature, not to put down a verbatim report on the interview. The same goes for facts gathered from research and for the thoughts you might have had for personal experience articles. Put the facts into a *readable* order, even if that is not the *natural* order.

The apparent exception to this rule is the type of feature that is written as a straight question and answer type of article, showing both the interviewer's questions and the interviewee's answers. At first sight this would appear to take the easy way out; all you apparently need to do is to transcribe the tape that was recorded at the time of the interview. In fact, it's not as easy as that. For a start, people tend to ramble in general speech. They don't actually talk in sentences—not the sort of sentences that look right on paper. So you have to tidy things up. The interview itself might have wandered from one point to another, starting on one line of thought, progressing elsewhere and then, when you or your subject suddenly remembered some fact that had been left out, returning to a question that had actually been asked ten minutes before. To transcribe that conversation to paper would make a messy article. So you have to run the questions and answers around, to link certain things that were actually said at different times into a single answer.

Of the two types of feature that can be written for a magazine, my personal view is that this is the less satisfactory. It always looks like the easy way out to me and, at the end of the day, rarely produces such an interesting article. That doesn't detract from the fact that certain magazines like to use the style and, as a freelance writer, you must give them what they want. But, given the choice, I'd always present the alternative.

Here, you write about your subject more fluently, bringing in the person you interviewed in different ways. You can use direct speech: *"I started to keep bees when I was eight years old,"* Jack Smith said. Or you can bring in the same quotes as indirect speech: *Jack Smith said that he started to keep bees when he was eight years old.* Or, a third alternative is to write from your own viewpoint, talking about the interviewee: *Jack Smith started keeping bees when he was eight years old.* And, of course, you can mix all three.

A whole page of writing in a magazine article without any quotes in it looks very grey and boring, but a feature that is nothing but quotes can look bitty. The ideal is to mix all three styles mentioned above to produce an interesting and readable piece of writing.

The intro

Every article has a beginning, a middle and an end. The beginning is the intro. This is the opening paragraph that kicks off your feature, and it is there to serve several purposes. First of all, it has to tell the reader what the feature is all about; secondly, it has to be intriguing enough to make the reader read on. Here's an intro:—

Jack Smith keeps bees. He has been doing so since he was eight years old. This is how he does it and why he decided to take up the hobby.

That's an intro of sorts. It tells the reader what the feature is all about, but it's not very exciting. It doesn't really encourage your reader to keep reading. What's needed is a little more intrigue. Try this:—

When eight-year-old Jack Smith was stung on the neck by a bee, it was the start of a love-hate relationship that, over the years, has introduced him to new friends, given a lot of pleasure and brought in a good deal of profit.

Straight away, we are intrigued. Why did a sting on the neck as a boy change Jack's life so much? We want to read on to find out the answers. So an intro must be brief and to the point. It must tell the reader that this is the sort of feature that he or she will want to read. It must give the facts of what the feature is all about, but it needs to keep something back, in order to hook readers and force them further into the feature. The intro should take the form of a short paragraph, certainly no longer than the examples shown above, but there is nothing to say that it should always consist of a single sentence. The experienced feature writer can get several short, sharp sentences into an intro. The first example did just that, but it was a boring paragraph. Here's a four sentence intro for our subject that is both interesting and intriguing:—

Jack Smith is a glutton for punishment. In the past twenty years or so, he has lost count of the number of times he has been stung. Not that he'd have it any other way. Stings are an occupational hazard, when you're a bee-keeper.

Once you get the knack, writing an intro comes almost as second nature. You begin to get a feeling for exactly what needs to be said, how to say it and —just as important—what needs to be left out. Even so, it is knack that needs to be acquired and it tends to come with experience. Right at the start, it can often seem impossible to come up with a good intro for your article and it must be said that I've seen experienced, professional writers sitting staring at a blank piece of paper for ages, just waiting for an intro to come. That, I find, is not the best way of going about things. If you can't write a good intro straight off, your best bet is to write a *bad* one. Having got over that hurdle, you can launch into your feature. By the time you have written half-a-dozen paragraphs, it's a fair bet that the intro you should have written in the first place will come to you, presented by the facts that you are now setting down on paper. At which point, you can go back to the beginning, scrub out your first thoughts and write your new intro.

The middle

The intro tells your reader what you're *about* to say. Now you have to actually say it. This is the point where you present your reader with the facts in the best possible way. So go back to your list and double-check to see if you have things in the right order. What you have to say should follow on naturally from the intro, but we should now see an expansion of what we already know. Here's where we learn the truth behind the who, what, how, where and why questions.

Earlier, I said that the only way to start typing was to start typing. Now I'm going to tell you that the only way to start writing is to start writing. Get everything down on paper in simple, easy to understand terms. Don't try to be clever when a simple approach will work better. Also, don't think that you have to write down *everything* that the person you interviewed said or for that matter, everything you feel or know about the subject. Sort out what is genuinely interesting to the reader and what might be waffle; keep to the facts as they apply to your subject and don't introduce new ideas that have little or no bearing on the feature in hand.

It's a good idea at this stage to try to see a theme behind your article. The theme is slightly different from the actual subject matter. In the example we've been looking at all along, the subject is a bee-keeper, the how, where, when and why he keeps bees. The *theme*, by comparison, might be buried in the fact that everyone told our bee-keeper that he'd never do it, but he did it just the same: one man's rebellion against advice to carry out an occupation or hobby that he believed in. Once you have established in your mind what that theme is, then it's a good idea to check every so often to make sure that you are following it and that what you are writing is in character with your theme. Doing that gives your feature more of an identity and, ultimately, makes it more readable.

Coming to the end

The way you end an article is almost as important as the way you begin it. When your reader gets to the end, he or she wants to feel satisfied. You need to leave them with some kind of impact, a punchline of some sort or something maybe that makes them laugh. Never end a feature with the corny . . . *so that's what makes Jack Smith keep bees for a hobby* sort of approach. Instead, find something about your subject that's truly worth saying, but which naturally falls towards the end of the story you're telling. One way is to look towards the future. Like this.

What's next on the bee-keeping horizon for Jack Smith? "Mass production," says Jack. "By the end of the year, I'll have 500 hives and be turning out honey at the rate of a pot a minute. I reckon I'll be a millionaire by the time I'm fifty." And all because a little boy of eight was stung on the neck by a bee.

That's the ideal kind of ending. It rounds things off but gives the impression that we haven't heard the last of this man.

Good endings are important, but they don't always come from something that happened at the end of the interview, or even the logical conclusions of your own thoughts.

Interviewed on the subject of bee-keeping, Jack Smith might well have mentioned his ambitions to be a millionaire by fifty about half way through the interview. But when you came to listen to your tape, or look through your notes, you should have seen that little quote as an ideal rounding-off point and so kept it to the end. Sometimes you'll get all the way through your feature with all the facts down on paper and then find you have no way to finish. A read through will often reveal a quote or a fact of some sort that looks as though it could fall naturally at the end. Then you can lift it out of the body of the article for use in the final paragraphs, making sure of course that you adjust the words so that they naturally flow over the hole you have made by removing some copy.

Writing the words

I've talked a lot so far about the importance of getting the facts down on paper and the way you should keep things simple, but I haven't mentioned how you actually go about preparing and presenting the words. That's where we are going now.

This is not a book on English grammar. Whole books have been written on that subject and to include all their information here would not only make this book far too large, it would also be largely unnecessary. I'm assuming, then, that you know the basics of how to write the English language: the way nouns, verbs, adjectives and adverbs go to make up clauses and sentences; the way sentences go together to make paragraphs. If you want to learn more about such matters, read one of the books on the subject. Perhaps the most popular book and one that tells you, in an easy to understand way, all you really need to know for the general application of the English language is *Fowler's Modern English Usage,* generally known simply as *Fowler.* It is published in paperback by Oxford University Press.

So I'm assuming you know the basics of writing straight-forward school textbook English. From there, I'm going to take you into the realms of turning it into journalese, destroying perhaps a few myths on the way and showing you a slightly different form of English grammar that is both acceptable and, indeed, often preferred by the world of publishing.

The first thing to remember is that the way your words *look* on paper can often be more important that what is actually grammatically correct. Take paragraphs, for instance. When you were at school, you were taught to examine an idea in one paragraph and not to start a new one until you had taken that idea to some form of conclusion. That's still the way it is in books, where the average width of type on a page is perhaps around 120mm. What does the *width* of the type on a page have to do with grammar? Quite a bit when it comes to journalism. At 120mm, you can afford to fill half a page with copy and the result is still easy to read—especially in a book which, generally speaking, people settle down to read with a lot more concentration than they do a magazine. The paragraph you are now reading contains 12 sentences and 210 words. Look at it, not for the words you have been reading, but for its shape on a page. It was quite easy to read, wasn't it? Its shape and size didn't put you off reading it, did it? Now let's transfer that line of thought to a magazine page.

Most magazines are A4 in size, across which type is arranged in columns. Unless we are talking about a particularly large size of type, running over a few words in perhaps a general introduction to a section of the magazine, it is rare to find only two columns on a page. Usually it's three or four. Three columns on an A4 page will usually be around 58mm in width, while four columns will give you about 44mm. In the first instance, the 210 words in that last paragraph would take up about one-third of the page in depth, while in the four-column setting, the same amount of words would make over half a page down one column. While there's nothing wrong with that grammatically, the effect is uneasy on the eye. It looks grey and boring and doesn't encourage the reader to start on it.

In magazine writing, it's the encouragement that's important, rather than the strict laws of English grammar. So the average paragraph is best arranged to consist of around 60 words, making it look better on the page. In some instances, that might be just a single sentence, in others it might be made up of three or four sentences. But what you must remember is that paragraphs are begun and ended for the sake of their appearance on the printed page, rather than for any laws of English grammar.

When it comes to putting the words down, simplicity of approach cannot be stressed enough. Imagine you are describing something to a friend and write it down in much the same way. Don't go for long, convoluted sentences, however clever or correct they might be grammatically, when two or even three sentences will make your point clearer. If you want an example of this kind of writing, look no further that this actual book. That's the way it has been written. In fact, look at those last three sentences. I could have written this: *Don't go for long, convoluted sentences, however clever or correct they might be grammatically, when two or even three sentences will make the point clearer, and if you want an example of this type of writing, look no further than this actual book, because that's the way it has been written.* Compare the two ways of saying the same thing and you'll soon see which is the easier, and the more *encouraging*, to read. Once you have got everything down the way you want it, go back and read it aloud. That's a good way of finding out if everything is clear, and it also shows you how the words flow.

Which brings us to scanning. Some sentences are just plain difficult to read—especially aloud. If you find you can't read them aloud with ease, then find another way of saying what needs to be said. Scan your sentences to give them a pleasant flow. Very often the alteration of an odd word here and there will make all the difference to the actual rhythm of a sentence. If the reader mentally stumbles over what you have written and needs to read it again and again to make sense of it, then you have failed.

Try to contrast the length of your sentences as you write. It can often be effective to write a fairly long sentence, followed by a much shorter one. Try it and see. (Re-read those last two sentences if you're in any doubt.)

Putting it on paper

Writing about the intro and ending of an article above, I mentioned going back to the beginning and re-writing, as well as lifting copy from the centre of the article and placing it at the end. Don't be afraid to do this. The first draft of your article is nothing precious, it's a working plan of the way the final draft will look. So don't be afraid to make mistakes, lift words, sentences or even complete paragraphs from one section and place them in another.

If you are working on a word processor, then you'll find this particularly easy to do, simply deleting paragraphs and inserting new ones, or taking one section and electronically shifting it to another place. Your first copy that comes off the printer should be as near perfect as it's possible to get. But assuming you are using a typewriter, then you should look upon your first copy as no more that a rough draft. Cross things out as you go along using the 'x' key on your keyboard, then make further corrections and alterations by hand when you have finished. Only when the feature is exactly the way you want it should you retype the final version.

If time is on your side, it is a good idea to leave retyping that final version for a few days after you have written the first one. Coming back to it fresh after a while will point out all sorts of extra places where you can see the possibility of improvement.

When you are checking you work this way, watch out for superfluous words. Beware especially of tautology. That's the unnecessary repetition of the same idea in different words. Don't write, for instance, about a "great big" mountain. If it's that big it's probably "enormous"—one word which gets the idea across in a neater way. Never be afraid to take words out of your article, providing the sense is still left intact. Sparse writing is the best kind there is for any form of journalism.

Beware too of using the same word too often in the same sentence or paragraph. For example, don't write something like, "In my opinion, the opinion of Mr. Smith is wrong." Instead, change it to, "In my *view* the opinion . . ." Little points like that can make all the difference to the way your feature is read, and they are the type of points that you don't always notice when you are actually writing. As soon as you stop writing and start reading, however, they stick out like a sore thumb. If you are stuck for a way to change words in this way, then invest in a thesaurus. This is a book like a dictionary, but instead of giving the meanings of words, it gives you all the many alternatives for just about every word you'll ever need to use. The most popular is undoubtedly *Roget's Thesaurus*, published in paperback by Penguin.

To help you acquire a writing style of your own, read articles and features in magazines that have been written by professional writers. Don't just read the words for the sake of their meaning, but look instead at the way the writer expresses himself on paper. Don't be afraid to copy someone else's style of writing and, from that, develop a style of your own.

Once you begin doing that, you'll see that many magazine writers seem to have scant regard for the basic laws of English grammar. At school, you learnt never to start a sentence with "And" or "But". You probably can't imagine how you could bring yourself to start a sentence with "Which". But I do it all the time. Which is no bad thing when it comes to getting information across. And if it works for me, it'll work for you. Another thing: don't feel that you must always stick to the subject-verb-object construction of sentences that is considered correct. Grammatically, every sentence should have a verb in it, but very often it can be extremely effective to write a sentence without. Like this one.

What all this adds up to is that, when it comes to writing journalistically, most of the rules are made to be broken. But don't go too far. Learn the rules before you break them, so that you know why you are breaking them. Then, when you do break them, do so for effect, not merely for the sake of it. Overdoing anything along these lines can become an annoyance very quickly, and the style you have adopted in order to attract the reader can just as easily turn him or her away.

A final point to keep in mind when you are actually committing words to paper is to make sure that you really do know their meaning. The English language is an ambiguous one and very often you'll find words don't mean what you think they do. Always work with a good dictionary at your side, along with your thesaurus and *Fowler* and, if in any doubt at all about the meaning of a word, look it up. If it doesn't mean what you thought it did, don't use it.

Even after you have written your final copy, it's naturally wise to look through it because there are bound to be a few places where you might want to make changes. These might be as simple and as straightforward as the correction of typing errors, or they might be a little more complicated, like the insertion or deletion of complete sentences. If you find a lot of alterations to make at this stage, for the sake of neatness and presentation, it's a good idea to re-type the whole page. But if your corrections are small and few, you can make them neatly with pen, using a system of printers marks that you'll find at the back of this book.

Writing titles

When you get to the end of your magazine article, you'll want to give it a title. Titles should be slick and to the point, never too long. To get an idea of what's needed, look at your chosen magazine to see how they use titles. Some are brief, no more than three or four words in length, others are much longer. Some are straightforward to the point of being boring, others are amusing, using puns or misquoting famous sayings. If you can match your title with the style of your target magazine, then it will obviously show the editor that you have studied his market and will go some way to helping you sell your feature. But don't worry if you can't think up anything which you consider to be slick enough.

The best advice here is not to try being too clever. Simply write a brief and to-the-point title that sums up the subject of your feature, and don't be disappointed if it gets changed by the magazine's editor or sub-editor. Titles follow style very closely and often you'll find that the magazine staff will write their own for your work automatically. Sticking to a straight title that merely sums up the article, then, is not only the easiest way out, it's very often the best too. At the end of the day, a bad title will never stop the sale of a good feature.

WRITING FOR NEWSPAPERS

**"Newspapers always excite curiosity. No one ever
lays one down without a feeling of disappointment."**
—Charles Lamb

Ask yourself this: why is a newspaper so called? Answer: because it brings you *news*. Obvious? Of course it is, but it's surprising how many would-be writers try to break into newspapers with stories and ideas that have little or nothing to do with anything that might even vaguely be called new. Because that's what news is all about. It's information about some thing, some person, some idea, some event about which the readers have not heard. Or, if the story being told revolves around something about which they *have* heard, then your words must produce a new angle, a fact that has hitherto been unknown.

Naturally, there are places where that basic underlying theme doesn't always hold true. The brief caption to a glamour picture on Page 3, for instance. But by and large, there is something new to be learnt from reading just about every story in a newspaper. And even that glamour picture caption will usually *purport* to tell you something about its busty subject that you never knew before.

There are several different types of newspaper, but by and large they all use three main types of copy: news stories, features and picture captions. Before looking at the way newspapers use each of these, let's examine first the different *types* of newspaper, because a knowledge of the type of paper you are aiming at will dictate how you write your story—and even if it is worth writing it at all!

Local newspapers

There are two types of local newspaper: the good old local rag that has been around for years and the freesheet, which is probably a lot younger but which, in many areas, is driving the more traditional local paper out of business. Both types are in business to make money, but the traditional local paper sees editorial as its strongest point. The advertisements are there to keep the costs down and to pay the wages of the staff, together with the paper's cover price, because this one is sold in local newsagents. The freesheets see advertising as their first concern and very often news is looked upon almost as an afterthought. The paper is pushed free through all the letterboxes in town, which is why they can claim a larger circulation, charge higher rates for the advertisements and give it away free. It's also why this type of paper is tending to overtake the older style.

Each has its own advantages for the freelance writer. The traditional paper, being more editorial-biased, might take your offer of work more seriously; the freesheet, being based around its advertising content, might be more desperate for editorial. To get an idea of your chances with either, take a serious look at each in your own home town. Having said that freesheets treat editorial as an afterthought, it must be said that a new breed is beginning to emerge these days which treats news every bit as importantly as its more traditional counterpart. If your local freesheet is one of these, then there could be room for you. But if it consists of little more than pages and pages of advertising with a flimsy front and back page of news around them, then you'll probably be better off with the other type of paper.

Local newspapers, in general, do not need a great deal from outsiders. Most are equipped with their own team of reporters for news and features. If you do have a good news story, it's a good bet that they won't let you write it yourself, but instead will send a reporter to interview you who will then write the story in the style that's needed by the paper. What you can sell here is feature material—articles that aren't actually hard news but which are about local people and events, reports on the activities of local clubs, drama or music criticisms (more usually known as 'crits') on local productions, even personal opinion pieces on matters of local interest.

It is rare that you will get such material accepted on spec, simply because the paper is not equipped to take such material on a regular basis the way a magazine usually is. Your best line of approach, therefore, is a personal one, straight to the editor. You'll find an address and usually a telephone number in the paper's imprint—a small area of type usually found at the bottom of the back page. Use this to make personal contact, explain what you have to offer and what you have in mind, emphasising what *you* can give the paper that the average reporter can't. A specialist knowledge of music, for instance, might get you a regular job reviewing local concerts; the same with drama.

One point worth bearing in mind is that local newspapers are extremely parochial. Each has its boundaries and the stories it prints are confined to people or places within those boundaries. That can work for and against you. Before submitting *anything* to a local paper, make sure that the point of your story has a strong *local* connection and that the locality you are talking about is definitely within its boundaries.

Where this narrow line of thinking can be of use to you is when you find a local story *outside* those boundaries. You might, for instance, be on holiday and come across a story that concerns someone who comes from the area of your local paper or perhaps who might once have lived there. That's when you can write a news story without fear of a local reporter turning up to take it away from you. By the same token, of course, remember that there are probably a lot of stories happening in and around your own area which, because the people concerned come from elsewhere, will be of interest to local newspapers *outside* your area. What's more, the stories we're talking about don't have to be that far outside the area. Most local newspaper staff work on expenses that are carefully watched over by a management who demands that those expenses don't take them further than the paper's boundaries. Just a few miles over the boundary and you might easily find you have the field to yourself—providing, of course, your story has that essential local angle.

Many freelances write the local newspaper off as a place without potential. In fact, providing you can offer the paper something that can be seen as a benefit to its readers, you can do quite well. But I advise the personal approach if you want to profit from what you write. Send in a report on your local sewing club and it might be used without credit or payment. But make it clear from the start you are in business to make money and that your work will help them sell papers and you could find yourself with regular, moderately-paid work.

National newspapers

Nationally-published newspapers break down mainly into the dailies that are published from Monday to Saturday and the Sundays. Most daily newspapers concentrate on hard news with features as a back-up, whereas the Sunday papers take a softer line, usually looking at the stories behind the big news events of the week, looking at those events maybe in more depth or from different angles, and often concentrating on feature material as much as they do on news. And, of course, some of them have their own colour supplements as well which are, in effect, complete news magazines.

When you come to look into a national newspaper, you need to think back to everything we said about market analysis when we were talking about the magazine market. Analysis of the market to see exactly what the magazine bought and why they bought it was the strong point being stressed in that section and it's just as important here. While most local newspapers are much the same as far as style and needs are concerned, national newspapers differ quite radically from one end of the market to the other. Some treat the news and the feature material they handle with great seriousness, dwelling only upon the weighty matters of the day or week. Others take a far more light-hearted approach, writing the important stories in a lighter and often more dramatic way. Also, they tend to run stories of a more frivolous nature, the kind that the more serious newspapers wouldn't find significant to their readers.

So before considering any form of submission to a national newspaper, choose the one you are aiming at first, then look at it carefully, analysing its content in exactly the same way as we spoke about earlier with magazines. That goes for the Sunday colour supplements too. It's then up to you to produce the kind of work that suits the style of your chosen newspaper.

As with local newspapers, the freelance writer stands a better chance with features than with news when it comes to national newspapers. Naturally, it is practically impossible to tell you what sort of subjects to look for, simply because newspapers cover *all* subjects and because their acceptance or rejection will often be influenced by their topicality as much as anything else. So with that in mind, fall back on your research and analysis techniques to discover what's needed.

What you will need to know is something about how to deal with a national newspaper. The biggest difference between this market and the national magazine market is deadlines. The copy you supply to a magazine will probably be in the newsagents in six weeks time. The copy you supply to a newspaper might be in the newsagents tomorrow—or, at the least, on Sunday morning. So time is of the essence. If you have in mind a feature idea that you feel can wait, then by all means write a letter, but if your idea is bang up to date, then don't delay. Use the telephone. Ask for the features desk if you are talking about features, or the news desk if you have a news story.

It is not impossible for a freelance writer to get a news story in the national press, but don't waste the time of the editors you have to deal with. Make sure you are certain in your mind that the story you have really is news—the type you see in the paper every day, not just something that is of interest only to yourself or people in your particular area. Sometimes the writer can make money out of such stories without even having to write them! Providing you have the facts, a national paper might easily be interested in writing the story themselves and paying you for the information. They might even pay you for a tip about a news story, gathering the facts and writing them for themselves. But if you feel you have all the facts and that you can write them down fast, then they might take the story from you as you have written it. All of this naturally assumes you really do have a good news story that is worth the paper running. We'll deal in a moment with ways of actually writing your copy, but let's assume here that it's written and ready to be given to the newspaper.

Start by telephoning the paper you have chosen and asking for the news desk. The man or woman who answers will be in a position to tell from a brief outline whether or not they are interested in your story. So tell them quickly and simply what the story is all about. Explain that you are a freelance writer and that you have the story ready written in front of you. If they don't want it, they'll tell you so there and then. If they like what they hear, they'll probably say something like, "I'm putting you over to copy." That means they're transferring you to the copy-taking department.

When you talk to "copy", state your name, address and daytime telephone number. Then read over your story slowly and clearly, explaining where punctuation marks occur throughout. Refer to full stops as "points" and when you start a new paragraph, merely say, "par." Don't talk about speech marks, say, "quote" at the places where they stop and start. Refer to question marks as "queries". The man or woman on the other end is listening to you and taking your copy down straight onto a typewriter. If he or she asks you to hold because they are "going over", that means they are changing to a new sheet of paper, and because newspaper copy is written on small pieces of paper—or "folios"—that might be more often than you expect.

When you have finished reading your story, tell the copy-taker that it "ends" and leave it at that. There's no time for idle chat in the newspaper world, so don't try to engage the copy-taker in conversation either before, during or after you have read your copy. And don't be put off if the person taking the copy sounds bored out of his skull—he probably is!

Provincial newspapers

A provincial paper is published daily, often in the evenings. It is a mixture of national and local in its approach, being published within set boundaries the way a local newspaper is, but using national news. Usually, it will give predominance in any one issue to the national stories of the day, but it will bend over backwards in an attempt to get local stories into its pages. Given a good local story, it will sometimes use it in preference to a well-known national one.

Such papers are naturally interested in local news, but it has to be *good*, top-quality local news. You won't see typical parochial stories here about the local Women's Institute. The set-up of such papers is very much larger than that of a normal local newspaper and, in the number of staff it employs and the way in which it handles news, it works like a small national. So by all means try a provincial paper with a good local news story or feature, but approach them as you would a national.

Types of story

We've touched briefly on news stories, features and captions, but so far we haven't looked into how each differs from the other. Let's remedy that right now.

A news story is one that concerns some topic of immediate news. It might be a light-hearted piece of news or it might be very important and topical. Either way, the story will be bang up to date. Getting what newspaper people call a nose for news is one of the most important aspects of this business and it's not an easy thing to learn. It's something for which you need a feel. But a good rule of thumb is to ask yourself genuinely if it is the sort of story which you, or someone you know, would find personally interesting. What constitutes a news story differs according to the exact circumstances of that story. For instance . . .

If a car crashes at the end of your street, that's not news.

If a plane crashes anywhere in the world, that is news.

If your nextdoor neighbour marries her third husband, that's not news.

If the star of a top-running soap opera marries her third husband, that is news.

If your nextdoor neighbour marries her third husband, while the two of them dangle from a helicopter, that's news.

If your dog gets run over, that's not news.

If the Queen's dog gets run over, that is news.

If a model, famous for regularly revealing her charms on Page 3 appears nude in *Playboy*, that's not news.

If an elegant female TV presenter who has only ever been seen before in demure, high-necked dresses appears nude in *Playboy*, that is news.

If a world-famous financier makes a million pounds on a business deal, that's not news.

If a dustman wins half-a-million pounds on the football pools, that is news.

Get the idea? It's not always the story that makes the news, so much as the combination of the story and the person to whom it happens. In other words, anything that is slightly out of the ordinary is news, even if—and sometimes *especially* if—the facts you are reporting would be perfectly ordinary in different circumstances.

A news feature follows much the same theory, but here we're not talking too much about something that is immediately topical. The *subject* might be topical, but the way the feature deals with it is different to the way the news story would handle the facts. The feature usually assumes that the reader has heard the original story and it is now going to bring you the facts behind the story, or perhaps expand in a more leisurely way on that story. A news feature might also deal with a current topic that needs greater breadth than can be given in a straight news story.

The subjects of features are always newsworthy, although they might not be new in the sense that the subject of a news story might be. When the reader comes to look at the feature, he or she will always learn something new, but it might not directly concern a topical or current event the way a news story does. It might, for instance, concern some new evidence that has come to light about World War II. There's nothing strictly new or newsy about the last war, but the facts around which this feature are built must be new.

Picture captions can be both news-biased and feature-biased. Once again, the overriding reason for their inclusion in a newspaper must be that they are bringing the reader something new and hitherto unknown. But in this case the picture stands as the more important factor, the words are there only to explain, to clarify and often merely to amuse. Just as with all other forms of newspaper journalism, however, the reason behind the picture's appearance in the paper must follow all the usual rules of what is and what is not news. If you are boarding a boat and your hat blows off, no one would ever think of trying to sell such a picture to a newspaper, but if the same thing happened to Prince Charles and a photographer was there to catch his look of impatience or surprise, he'd have the perfect picture for a sale—and the need for a picture caption.

Newspaper style

Let's turn our attention now to writing the words. If you've read the chapter on writing for magazines, you'll already be on your way to knowing the basics of putting words down on paper in a journalistic way. What you need to do now is to take that information a few steps further, learning how to adapt it for use in newspapers.

The watchword with newspaper style is *brevity*. Stories should always be written in the shortest way possible. There are two good reasons for this. The first is that space is always at a premium. The second is that the average newspaper reader has a very short attention span. He reads a little of one story, skips to the end, goes on to another, darts about all over the page, reading what catches his eye, rather than tackling the words in the slower and more methodical way of a magazine reader.

A page lead in a tabloid newspaper—that's the biggest and most important story on the page—is rarely more than around 300-350 words. Other stories say what they have to say in as little as 150 words or even 50 words. Sentences are short and sharp, paragraphs containing only a few sentences each. Remember what I said earlier about the presentation of the written word and the way it must *look* interesting on the page? That's even more important in newspapers where each column might be as little as 40mm across. Fill half a column with solid text and the reader won't want to know. Break it up into half-a-dozen paragraphs and the copy will look more inviting to read.

This style applies to all forms of newspaper writing, whether we're talking about a news story, a feature or a picture caption. Keep it brief and write it in a way that uses the fewest amount of words. Once you've written it, go through your copy and remove all unnecessary words. It's amazing how much you can tighten copy, just by changing around a few words and, removing the word "the". For example . . .

Fred Smith, the Director General of the BBC said today that the cost of a TV licence would soon be the highest ever.

Now try this...

BBC Director General, Fred Smith, said today that TV licence costs would soon hit a new high.

That's six words cut out of 23 - just over a quarter of them in fact. Add that up throughout a 300-word story and you can soon see how much space can be saved.

Newspaper writing must be punchy. As you write, always think in terms of a reader who is in a hurry and whose attention must be kept at all costs. The moment your story starts to look boring, he'll turn the page and do the crossword instead. Everything we discussed earlier about intros goes double for newspaper writing. They really are there to grab your reader and *make* him read on. When you come to write the story, look at your facts, pick out the most important or most controversial and get them up there in the intro.

Do everything for impact. Don't be afraid to turn the laws of grammar on their head if you feel that doing so will keep the reader reading. That includes starting sentences and paragraphs with words like *and, but, so, which, because;* even writing paragraphs that consist of just a few words. Like this...

Joe Bloggs thought his luck had changed the night a beautiful girl knocked on his door and asked for help.

How wrong he was!

Because once inside the house, and in the light of the hall, the damsel in distress turned out to be no lady. Off came the wig, out came a gun and Joe found himself held at gunpoint as the intruder ransacked the house and escaped with over £600 in cash.

Written on this page, the shape of those sentences looks all wrong, but in a narrow newspaper column, they would look fine. Also notice the way the intro is written to practically compel the reader to keep reading. What would follow in a story like this would probably be an account of a court case and, in all probability, the average reader would never get to the end of it. Five minutes after he has read the story, he won't even remember the name of the bogus burglar. But for the few paragraphs at the start, the story held his attention and gave him something he found worth reading.

Perhaps the very best way to learn how to write newspaper copy is to read it. But not in the way you normally read a newspaper. Read it instead to see exactly how sentences are constructed in short, sharp paragraphs, how the intro grabs the reader, how all unnecessary words are eliminated and how the average story is "punched up" to make it as readable as possible. If you want to write for newspapers, you can do no worse than blatantly copy the style you see in the paper on your breakfast table every morning.

Headlines and crossheads

In the chapter on magazine writing, we looked at the relative unimportance of supplying the perfect title for a feature. With newspaper stories, it is even less important. Newspaper stories don't even have titles— they have headlines, and they are written exclusively by the paper's sub-editors.

A good headline needs to do more than give a title to the story. It needs to get the reader's attention, even more than the intro. It must tell the story in only a few words without giving away too much, and so encourage the reader to make the effort to start on the story itself. According to the way the page of the paper has been designed, it has to be in a certain kind of type and fit a certain space, both in width and in its depth. Even if you do manage to write a good newspaper headline, it's a fair bet that it won't fit the space being planned for it in the typeface that has been assigned. All of which means that headline writing is best left to the paper's sub-editor and you, as a freelance writer, needn't worry about supplying one of your own.

And while we're at it, forget the crossheads too. They're those single words in bold type that you see interspersed throughout the copy. They too are put there by the sub-editor and are used for the sake of layout, preventing a long story from looking too boring on the page, rather than to bring the reader any real information.

WRITING A BOOK

"Making books is a skilled trade, like making clocks."
—Jean de la Bruyere

Who was it who said, "Everyone has a book in him"? The answer is most people at some time or another, especially those currently involved in trying to write a book. The quote has probably been derived from something the author Somerset Maughan once said and there is a sting in the tail that doesn't usually get quoted. What Maughan actually said was, "There is an impression abroad that everyone has it in him to write a book; but if by this is implied a good book, the impression is false."

Personally, I prefer the quote that has been attributed to comedian Peter Cook who, indulging in small talk at a party is said to have asked someone what he was working on at that time. "Writing a book," said the party-goer. "Neither am I," replied Cook.

I defy anyone who has the slightest interest in writing to deny that they haven't thought about writing a book at some stage. In fact, I'd be willing to bet that if you have enough interest to have bought *this* book, then you have gone further; you've actually started putting words down on paper. The question is, how far have you progressed, and are you ever going to finish it?

The fact is that writing a book is hard work. Unlike a magazine or newspaper article that can be researched and written fairly fast—in as little as an hour at times—a book needs dedication and a lot of time, especially so since the vast majority of book writers work in their spare moments, in evenings and at weekends. I'm a full-time freelance writer who tries desperately (and often without success) not to be working after six o'clock at night or at weekends, and yet, putting time aside at regular intervals during my daily work, the book you are now reading still took close to a year to write.

The average book has a minimum of 50,000 words in it and often a lot more. So before you even start to write a book, you've really got to *want* to write it. Because, believe me, once you have the first couple of chapters under your belt, the novelty begins to wear off, and all the rest is hard slog.

Fact or fiction?

Think about book-writing and your thoughts probably turn to novels. I'm not going to knock it. There is no point in my telling you that you don't stand a chance of getting a novel published, because novels by first-time authors are being accepted for publication all the time. The problem is that for every one that is accepted, hundreds are turned away, and although you *might* have the talent and willpower to produce an overnight best-seller, the *likelihood* is that you'll fail. Prove me wrong and I'll be delighted to hear from you, but throughout this book, I have been determined not to attempt to sell dreams. I don't want to fool you into thinking you can suddenly become rich and famous from your writing. Stick with me and I'll tell you the reality of what's possible, rather than what sounds good but which is, in fact, improbable. With that in mind, let's stick to non-fiction.

Find your subject

To start writing a book, you need two things: a subject and a publisher who is interested in that subject. In this respect, books are a lot like specialist magazines. There is no point in trying to write a book on a subject that is already well-known to everyone. Just as with a magazine article, you need a new angle; you should aim to bring new information to the reader. To that end, you need to find a subject that is popular, but about which you have something new to say. Good examples of such thinking are the numerous books that are published each year on topics like gardening, cooking, photography, the supernatural ... in fact anything and everything which has a general interest to the public at large.

Previously, when we were talking about looking for subjects for magazine articles, I said that although it is a good thing to write essentially about what you know, it wasn't strictly necessary because you could always start researching and learning about new subjects. The same holds largely true about finding a subject for a book. But in this case, I would actually give preference to starting off with a subject that you know a good deal about. The fact is that with magazine articles, you can soon exhaust your own knowledge and be forced into moving on to new areas. On the other hand, you will write far fewer books than you will magazine articles and so you can afford to restrict the number of different subjects on which you write. Also the fact that you know a good deal about your subject means that you will be in a far better position to cover it in the sort of depth that just wouldn't be possible in a magazine feature.

Don't think, however, that you need not do your research. Once you have picked your subject, you should analyse your own knowledge of it in your mind. Do you know no more than the man in the street, or the average knowledgeable amateur, on your subject? Don't forget that the person who buys your book could easily already know a good deal about your subject and is buying the book only to increase that knowledge. So sort out for yourself what you do and don't know about your chosen topic. Examine the facts to see what gaps there are in your own education and then set out to fill those gaps.

You can do that by all the methods that we have already covered in the section on researching a magazine article. Interviews, publicity offices, other text books and personal experience all come into play when you start to research, but obviously you'll need a lot more research and better-ordered notes than you had when you wrote for a magazine. The average magazine article might easily be written from notes gathered from a single interview, or even from facts held inside your head. But to sustain interest throughout a book, you need a lot more research. It's best, then, to sit down and plan out the way you want your book to go even before you start your research.

Planning a book

The joy of writing a book is the sheer *depth* that you can give to your subject; the way you can cover it from all the angles. So often, with a magazine article, you are writing to a tight brief as far as the number of words are concerned and that, in turn, restricts how much you can put into the article. But with a book, you have no such restrictions. You are free to explore all the different aspects of your subject.

Nevertheless, you need a little self-imposed restraint. Don't use this fact as an excuse for rambling all over the place, away from the subject and back again without any real plan of action. Despite the fact that you have far more words to play with, your books should still be written in a tight way, keeping certain facts together and finishing one line of thought before you start another.

Everyone has a different method of making a start, but my way, which is one that I pass on to you, is to start with a blank sheet of paper. Having chosen the subject that you are going to write about, you can now jot down words or phrases that sum up various aspects of your subject. From this, you will soon see some form of plan developing and from that you can start to draw up a more orderly list of what the book needs to contain. Now you can start to arrange it into chapters. One of the difficulties you'll find here is that certain items might seem to be applicable to more than one chapter and that's where you'll need to think matters through as logically as possible. Despite the fact that you have so many words to play with, there is absolutely no point in saying the same thing twice or more. So if you do come up against this problem, try to arrange matters so that the topic you will have to refer to falls in an early chapter and can then be referred to or adapted in later chapters.

A perfect example of this line of thinking can be seen in this very book. I knew when I came to plan it that I would have to talk about research when it came to magazines, newspapers and books. I got over this problem by writing a whole chapter on research as it applies to magazines and I have continually referred to that in later chapters. A similar problem arose when I thought about including something on the techniques of actually putting words down on paper. When I planned the shape of the book, I knew that I would have something basic to say and that those basics could then be adapted and changed to work for magazines, newspapers and books. So I started off by talking about the techniques of writing a magazine article, adapted those facts and showed how they needed to be changed for newspapers and, shortly, we'll be looking at those same basics afresh for the way they apply to books. This is something that could never have come out of sitting straight down and beginning to write without any real plan of action, because I would soon have got myself into difficulties of repetition. It came out of getting a strong plan together before I even started to write the first chapter.

That's just one of the problems that can be solved by the making of a plan. Another is the organisation of chapters into logical order. Let's stay with the way this actual book was conceived and written, because doing so will give you a very real practical insight into the tasks involved. When I was writing down words and phrases on that first blank sheet of paper, one of the first that I wrote down was "presentation", because I knew how important that is to successful sales. Later, I wrote down "copyright". When I came to turn these random words and phrases into chapters, I saw how logically those two items go together. I also saw that it was a logical thing to put at the end of the book, despite the fact that it was one of the first things I thought of.

About half-way through the plan I was drawing up on the various types of writing, I suddenly thought that I ought to cover something on actual equipment, telling newcomers about typewriters and other tools of the trade. When I came to make my list of chapters, that went right up the front —something to start with before getting down to actual writing.

From this way of thinking, you can see how the book was planned in a logical progression. Take a look back at the contents page to remind yourself of what has gone before and to see what is yet to come. You'll see that after an introduction, we go logically through equipment, markets, research and writing for the major market sector that concerns magazines, before branching out into newspapers, books and then onto a different aspect altogether in fiction, finishing with the point where *you* will finish— with the actual submission of your work and what follows. The shape of this book didn't come by chance. It came from planning, and it's naturally the same with any book on any subject that you tackle.

By now, you should at least have a set of chapter headings. Those are the bones on which you add the meat. So under each chapter heading, you can write ideas and topics that you will be covering in that chapter, once again ensuring that you are proceeding in a logical direction and that you are not repeating yourself throughout the book. You can also swop items about. Very often, something that you originally planned to be in one chapter will be seen to work better in another one.

When you come to make these notes, write down *everything* that needs to be said about each topic, including details that you still have to check out. This will give you another indication of what you need to research and what you can pluck from your own knowledge. Not that you have to stick religiously to your list. Very often, once you start to write, you'll realise that something you noted down for later in the book works better in an earlier chapter, and vice versa. If that happens, don't fight it. Providing the change works logically in the context of what you are writing, then go with it—but change your list accordingly, so you'll know how it affects any later chapters.

Writing a book is such a lengthy occupation that you should never rely on memory alone to tell you what has gone before or what needs to come up in the future. Always keep notes of where you've been and where you are going if you want to produce a well-planned piece of writing.

Writing the words

Over the past chapters, we've dealt quite closely with actually putting words down on paper, so we needn't go too far into details here. Let's just look at some of the differences between words in books and those that appear in newspapers or magazines.

Of the two, the closer comparison is with magazines, newspaper style being too short and abrupt for a book reader. The difference is that you no longer have to think quite so much of your words in terms of their shape or appearance on a page. The person who reads a book usually does so with much more concentration than the person who reads a newspaper or magazine. You don't have to "hook" your reader in the same way. It's a good idea to start off the book—and each chapter too—with a good intro, the sort of thing that pulls the reader into the chapter, but you don't need to get *all* the facts up there in the first paragraph, the way you might in a news item or magazine feature. Neither do you need to be so abrupt. You can take time to construct a good sentence, rather than trying to make everything short and sharp the way you did before. Paragraphs can be longer, fully exploring certain themes before moving on. Now when you move to a new paragraph, you can do so for grammatical reasons, but you shouldn't overlook the way you can still write for effect. The training you have given yourself learning about magazines and newspapers will stand you in good stead for book writing, but you can afford to relax a little and bring a better sense of style to your writing.

Try to think of each chapter of a book as an extra-long magazine feature. Start with an intro that gives some indication of what's to follow, cover your facts thoroughly in the coming pages and round off with a tight ending, something which gives a full stop to that section and tells the reader that he or she has reached the end of that chapter, preparing them mentally for the start of the next.

Finding a publisher

Look in the classified advertisements of the national press and you'll see adverts placed by publishers who appear, from what they say, to be dying for your words. Just send them a manuscript and they'll turn it into a book, they seem to be saying. It's a tempting offer, but it's one you should ignore. Look into matters further and you'll usually find that these adverts have been placed by what are known as vanity publishers. There is absolutely nothing unlawful or even unethical about what they are doing, but placing your work with them will do you little good as an author. In fact, they are merely printers who will take a manuscript and turn it into a book. Naturally, they'll then charge you for it and deliver to you as many books as you require. It's up to you how you sell them.

With certain specialist works, or for books that you know you have a ready market for, the exercise might be worth your while. But if you are serious about writing a book, you should go to a proper, recognised publisher.

Perhaps because of the existence of vanity publishers, many would-be authors hold the mistaken belief that they have to pay a publisher to handle their work. In fact, nothing could be further from the truth. A reputable publisher will take your work only if he thinks he has a good chance of making money from it—and so *he* pays *you*. It's then his job to get the book printed and sold.

Finding the right publisher for your book is a lot like finding the right magazine for your feature. Like magazines, different publishers specialise in different subjects, so your main task is to find one that is prepared to consider the subject of your proposed book. You can do that by looking around the book shops, finding books that deal with your subject without actually covering the ground that your book might be looking at. All publishers have their name and address printed in their books, usually on an early left-hand page. Alternatively, you'll find a list of publishers, together with their addresses, names to contact and the subjects with which they deal, listed in the *Writers' and Artists' Yearbook,* published annually by A&C Black.

One factor that a newcomer to book publishing might not be immediately aware of is the fact that often the writer—and the photographer too for that matter—doesn't always deal direct with the publisher. Sometimes a packager is involved. A book packager is a sort of middle man who gets all the necessary parts of a book together and then sells the finished product straight to a publisher to be distributed under his name. The packager might buy words from one person, pictures from another, organise typesetting from one place, colour reproductions from another, and have it actually printed somewhere else again. That's his job and, if your chosen publisher uses packagers a lot, you as an author will be better off dealing with the packager. If a packager was involved in the production of a book, you'll see his name printed with the publisher's, usually under a credit that says something like, "Designed and produced by . . ."

Like publishers, you'll find a list of packagers published in the *Writers and Artists Yearbook,* along with names, addresses and, once again, the subjects in which they specialise. Providing you stick to packagers who handle your chosen subjects, you are often better off dealing with one, rather than with a publisher. That's because the packager will already be known to several publishers for whom he regularly works and, once he has agreed that your book has potential, he will do the searching round to find the right place to have it published. Also, there's a good chance that he will have connections with overseas publishers too, so that you stand a chance of having your book published both at home and abroad, whereas a straight publisher might handle only the UK side of things.

Making the approach

Whether you are dealing with a conventional publisher or with a packager, your initial line of approach is much the same. Make sure you start by getting an actual name, to whom you will be writing. The man or woman you want to approach is the commissioning editor and if the publisher is large, there might be more than one, each specialising in a different subject. So before making any submission, telephone the publisher and enquire about the name of the person you are going to approach. You'll need to do this if you have taken an address and telephone number from an actual book, but it's wise to do it too if you are taking details from the *Yearbook.* Despite the fact that names of commissioning editors are included, things might have changed since the directory was published. So double check.

Once you know who to approach, write a brief letter, inquiring if the publishing house would be interested in your proposed book. Make sure you include the following details:—

1. A brief outline of the subject and the way you aim to tackle it.
2. Why you feel such a book is needed.
3. Any other similar books that you know of already on the market.
4. Why your book is superior to, or better than, those other books.

Each of these points is very important to the publisher when he is considering your proposal and, when you come to map out your ideas, it's as well to keep in mind that you have to justify these various points to the publisher. It's little use trying to fool him into publishing your book when you know full well that there is an identical one already on the market. So find reasons why your work is different and tell your publisher what they are.

If the publisher or the packager to whom you have written feels there could be something worthwhile in your ideas, he will ask you to take things one step further. There is a chance that he might ask you to write the whole book and submit it on spec, but it's more likely that he'll ask for a more detailed sample of your work. The usual request is for a synopsis and a sample chapter. The synopsis should consist of a series of chapter headings with brief notes on what you plan to include in each. The sample chapter should be written exactly the way you visualise it appearing in the finished book. It doesn't necessarily have to be the *first* chapter of your book, just so long as it is representative of the overall work.

If the publisher or packager likes this, you might then proceed to contract. Alternatively, if he is not quite certain of you or your work, he might possibly ask for another chapter on spec. Or if he thinks the work has potential but that it isn't quite right, he might make suggestions about how you can alter it, either the actual writing style or the layout of chapters. He might, equally, reject the whole thing at this stage, in which case you are back to square one, leaving you to rethink your ideas or maybe try another publisher.

Assuming the publisher or packager likes what he sees, then you're on your way. At that point you should get a contract.

The terms of a contract

There are two ways to be paid for a book. One is as a lump sum, the way you would be paid for an article in a magazine; the other is by a system of royalties. Each has its merits and its disadvantages.

With the lump sum method of payment, you get a good fee early on, but it's probably the last you'll see of any money for the work you've done. It will be a good, worthwhile fee, but it will be for *everything*. It will probably be the same fee, however many books are printed and however many different countries your work is published in. This is the sort of deal that packagers usually offer and it's a good way of making a large sum of money fast. It's worth enquiring, however, if the contract you are given can be so written as to pay you a further percentage of that first fee, each time the book is reprinted. Whether or not you get an agreement on that will largely depend on the amount paid in the first instance.

My own experience and advice on this method of payment is that it is worth it if you are writing on a subject that could be quickly dated and which you can write fairly fast without too much bother. After all, the faster you write, the more attractive the fee becomes and, when you work it out on an hourly rate, you'll probably discover that you are being paid very well indeed. The fee is usually paid in three instalments—one on commissioning of the manuscript and as soon as you sign the contract, a second on acceptance of the manuscript and a third on publication of the book.

If, on the other hand, you are working on a book that has been laborious to write and which you have put many hours into, and further, if this is the type of book that looks like it could keep on selling year after year, then it is probably better to go for the second option, should it be offered. In this, you are paid a royalty. That's a set amount for every book sold. The amount will be determined by the contract, but for a newcomer to book writing it will probably be around 10 per cent of the book's cover price for a hardback and about eight-and-a-half per cent of its price for a paperback. Against this, you will be given an advance. That is a set sum in advance of the royalties and which will be deducted from your first royalty payment. The advance is usually paid in two instalments, the first either on signing the contract or on acceptance of the manuscript, the second on publication of the book. Thereafter, once the book has been published, you will receive your royalties at regular intervals, every six months in the case of most publishers.

The amounts paid will be small, compared to that lump sum offered in the first way of paying, but they will keep coming, and the nice thing about this method of payment is that you keep getting paid years after the book has been published and the hard work of writing it is long forgotten.

Other terms that you will find laid out in the contract could include an option for the publisher to act as your agent in selling the book overseas, in which case you will be entitled to another royalty at a different rate. You might also see references to selling off large numbers of the book at reduced costs, in which case you will be entitled to a percentage of the lump sum received by the publisher. This is nothing to worry about. It probably applies to a deal the publisher has done with a book club who have offered to buy a set amount. This allows the publisher to increase the print run which, in turn, reduces the actual cost of each book. It is therefore worthwhile selling off those books at what appears to be a vastly reduced rate, just for the sake of reducing overall costs—and you will still make a small sum that you would not otherwise have seen.

All of these terms will be clearly set out in the contract, which you should read carefully before signing. A publisher's contract, at first sight, can look like a daunting document, full of legal jargon, but once you take the time to study it carefully, you'll find everything quite straightforward and easy to understand, and if you have any worries or difficulties, your newfound friend the commissioning editor will be only to pleased to explain what the various clauses mean to each of you.

WORDS AND PICTURES

"You press the button, and we do the rest."
—vintage Kodak advertisement

If you've taken a careful note of everything that has gone before, you now stand a good chance of starting to sell what you write. If you want to stand an even *better* chance, add some pictures. The fact is that there are a lot of freelance writers about selling their work to all the markets we've mentioned so far. There are a lot of freelance photographers around too, and they make regular sales with their pictures. But speak to any editor and you'll hear how rare it is for a freelance to supply both words and pictures. As such, freelances who can do both immediately better their chances of success. Not that you need to be a photographer to supply pictures with your words. You don't even have to be a top-notch professional photographer to *take* the sort of pictures we're talking about here.

The difference between you and a professional photographer is that the latter goes out specifically to take pictures that sell in their own right for markets like calendars, magazine covers, fashion houses, etc. The pictures you are going to take, or merely supply, would rarely make sales for their own sakes. They are not pictures so much as illustrations that add emphasis to your words. Most of them would seem pretty pointless without the words in fact. Such pictures are not difficult to take, even for someone who has never before used a camera. We'll come back to the techniques needed in a moment, but first let's look at the matter from a different angle.

Pictures without a camera

Earlier, we spoke about the power of the press or public relations office, how such departments are willing to give out information of products that will get them some free publicity in return. The same goes for pictures. If you are working on a project that needs the use of a PR department, then don't be afraid to ask them for pictures. They usually have files of them ready and waiting for that purpose and they won't charge you for them.

The same might easily go for the person you are interviewing in relation to a certain piece of information. The person concerned might easily have his or her own picture that is relevant to your article, and he or she might well be willing to loan it to you for the sake of the article. A word of warning here, though. The pictures from PR departments are taken specifically for publicity use and, if they give you a set, they will already own the copyright, which they will allow you to use for the sake of publicity. But if you borrow a picture from a private individual, then the copyright theoretically belongs to the photographer who took the picture in the first place, unless it was commissioned by the person you are dealing with, in which case that person owns the copyright and is at liberty to give you permission to use it. If that's not the case, the original photographer might object to having his work appear in print without a fee or credit. So check that little matter out before you start using other people's pictures for your own purposes.

Photo libraries are another place where you can get pictures to illustrate your words. For a list of all the major agencies in the UK and the sort of work they keep on file, write to the British Association of Picture Libraries and Agencies. For a small fee, they'll send you a list of all their members. You'll find BAPLA at PO Box 4, Andoversford, Nr. Cheltenham, Gloucestershire GL54 4JS. Alternatively, a list of leading libraries can be found in the *Freeelance Photographer's Market Handbook,* which was mentioned earlier and is available from BFP Books.

If you are buying from a picture agency, it is not a good idea to turn up at the front door without an appointment. A telephone call in advance, alerting the agency to who you are and what you need, will usually result in an invitation to come and look through their files. On arrival, you will be shown a selection of pictures from what is often a vast stock and, providing they accept you as a genuine buyer, they will allow you to take a selection away on spec, providing you sign for their release. That allows you to take a closer look at your selection when you get them home and to make a final choice of the picture or pictures that you want to use. Once you have made that choice, return all the other pictures, either personally or by registered mail. And take great care of them while they are in your possession. If you read the small print of that document you have signed, you'll see that you have undertaken to pay a lot of money per picture for any loss or damage that occurs while they are in your care. You'll also see that the agency reserves the right to charge you a set amount per picture per week for retaining them longer than necessary.

Naturally you have to pay a picture agency for use of their pictures and in many cases the costs are not cheap, but if the picture is right and if the market you are working for will allow you to pass the costs on to them, extra to your own fee as a writer, then the exercise can be worth it. But because of the costs involved and because of the responsibility you have to the agency, it is a good idea to make sure you have a sale guaranteed before getting involved with buying pictures this way. It is rarely a good idea to supply agency pictures with an article that has been written and submitted on spec.

The local newspaper is also a good place to come by pictures. If you have seen one used that would seem to be appropriate to your words (perhaps the feature you are writing was even inspired by an item in the paper in the first place), then contact their picture sales department. Legally, of course, they own the copyright, and that applies even if you do a private deal with the paper's photographer, so watch your step. But if you explain why you need the picture and how you plan to use it, you'll probably find they are happy to let you have a print, providing you credit the paper in the caption.

Perhaps the best way for a non-photographer to supply pictures is to team up with a real photographer. You can commission a professional to carry out any job for you, but before you let yourself in for such an expense, you must be pretty sure of your market and your chances of a sale —and sure of the fee that you and the photographer are going to get. A better bet is to team up with a part-time professional or a good amateur who is keen to get his or her work published. The fact that you can supply words to the photographer's pictures will increase his or her chances of success, so that the exercise could easily be mutually beneficial.

This is one place where it might be worth getting to know the local newspaper photographer. The pictures he takes for his newspaper are their copyright, but any he takes in his own time are his and he might be willing to work with you on various projects. Alternatively, why not try your local photographic society? Most members will be competent enough to take the kind of pictures you need and, once again, you should find no shortage of takers for your offer. The good thing about working this way is that the two of you can dream up ideas and agree to work on spec. That way, the photographer is taking as much risk with his time and materials as you are. If an idea doesn't come off, you don't owe anyone anything; if it sells, you can split the fee.

Perhaps the *very* best way to get the sort of pictures you need—and to increase your fee at the same time—is to take your own. If you have a knowledge of amateur or even professional photography, you can skip the next bit. But if you are a raw beginner, starting from scratch, to whom cameras are a total mystery, don't despair. Read on . . .

Choosing a camera

Look into any camera dealer's window and you will be totally confused by the number of different models, prices and specifications. But if you keep in mind exactly what you need a camera for, then we can easily begin a process of elimination.

The three most popular types of camera that you'll see in that window, or on the dealer's shelves, are 35mm compacts, 35mm single lens reflexes and rollfilm cameras. Start off by discounting the last kind. These are the rather bulky models that take 120 rollfilm and produce medium format negatives or slides in sizes that range from 6 x 4.5 cm, through 6 x 6 cm, up to 6 x 7 cm and even, on a few models, 6 x 9 cm. For the freelance *photographer*, they are very useful, simply because certain picture-buying markets refuse to accept smaller sizes for reproduction. But for the freelance writer, concerned only with adding illustrations to articles, then a 35mm camera makes far more sense, in terms of cost and in ease of use.

The "35mm" in the camera's description refers to the size of film it takes, and that's the same for any type or model of 35mm camera. We'll come back to film in a moment, but first let's look at the two main types of camera.

The first is the 35mm compact. This is a small camera, usually about the size of your outstretched hand, and it is typified by its high degree of automation. On most compacts, everything that *can* be automated *has* been automated. So exposure is handled for you automatically and so too is focus on the majority of models. As you press the shutter button, the picture is taken and the film automatically wound to the next frame, so there is no danger of forgetting to wind on. Most compacts have a flashgun built into them and on some models the flash even turns itself on automatically when the light levels are too low for normal photography.

At first sight, the 35mm compact camera might seem the obvious choice for the freelance writer in search of easy illustrations to articles. In fact, it can be used for many types of illustrations, but it does have its drawbacks. Most compacts have what is known as a semi-wide-angle lens fitted as standard. This means that it gives a wider view of the subject then you actually see with the human eye and although the viewfinder tells you what you are getting on film, it can still fool you into taking a wider view than you might have intended. The result is a subject that can often appear too small in the picture area. The same lens can also distort the image slightly if you do try to move in too close to the subject. So compacts are fine for subjects like landscapes, which might help you to illustrate articles on the countryside, or perhaps for certain types of travel feature. But for an article on something like a craftsman at work, in which you might want to move in close and be extra-precise about the exact picture you are getting on film, a compact can sometimes let you down.

For that reason, it's often a better bet to go straightaway for the second alternative: the 35mm single lens reflex. An SLR is so called because the viewfinder system actually looks through the lens, by way of a mirror that automatically flips up at the moment of exposure, allowing the same image to be recorded on the film. To the uninitiated, an SLR can look a little forbidding—all knobs, levers and dials that will take half a lifetime to learn the use of. At one time, that was very much the case, and only dedicated amateur and professional photographers bought this type of camera. Today, things are a little different. Computerized automation has arrived in cameras, making even the most complicated easy to use.

It is not the intention of this book to teach the reader the techniques of photography, but suffice it to say that there are three main factors on any camera that need to be taken into account to get good pictures—the focus, the aperture and the shutter speed. The first of these controls the sharpness of the picture; the other two look after exposure. The dedicated photographer will want to have all of these factors under his or her own personal control, and so will often go for a manually-operated camera. But for the writer who merely wants to add pictures to words, it is better to think in terms of relying more on automation.

Most camera manufacturers have in their ranges at least one SLR—and usually more than one—that uses what's called programmed automation. Some, in fact, are operated *only* in the program mode, but most offer program alongside other forms of automation, as well as providing the option for manual override. This type of camera is probably the best bet for the type of photography we have in mind. With the exposure mode button set on "program", both shutter speed and aperture are automatically selected and set by the camera, according to the level of light. You can use this mode for much of your photography, but as you become more proficient, and probably more interested in photography as a hobby in itself, then you can begin to learn to use the other modes too.

The only other control you need worry about is the focus. More and more this too is becoming automated on SLRs, but focusing is not difficult to work manually, even for the rawest beginner. The fact that the camera's viewfinder is actually looking through the lens on an SLR means that you can see the picture just the way it will appear on film and, with a little practice, focusing becomes second-nature.

Camera accessories

There are a few accessories that will be useful to you, once you have learnt the basics of camera use. There are also a whole lot more that might be tempting, but which might be just a waste of money.

A strong advantage of using a single lens reflex camera is the way it allows you to interchange lenses. The one that comes with the camera is called the standard lens and its view approximates what you see with the human eye. You can interchange this with wide-angle lenses that allow you to take in more at the sides, top and bottom of your picture, or telephoto lenses which bring far subjects closer. Lenses are designated by focal lengths. The standard is usually 50mm. Wide-angles have designations like 35mm, 28mm, 24mm, 16mm; the lower the number, the wider the view. Telephotos have longer focal lengths like 100mm, 135mm, 200mm, 500; the higher the number, the greater the magnification. A zoom lens has a range of focal lengths than can be changed according to the effect you want. They have ranges like 28-85mm, 70-210mm, 100-300mm, etc. When you first start out, and for much of the work we are referring to here, you'll need little more than the standard lens. If you do find the use for extra lenses, don't be too ambitious. Don't, for instance, go for a super-long telephoto just for the novelty of bringing far objects much closer to the camera. A good starting point is to go for a wide-angle lens of 28mm and medium-to-long telephoto zoom of around 70-210mm.

A small flashgun can also be handy for times when light levels are low or when you want to shoot indoors. Once again, computer technology has made flash photography child's play these days. As a beginner, buy a dedicated flashgun, designed for your own make of camera. Once this is fitted into the hot-shoe on the top of the camera body, a series of electronic connections are made which allow the gun and the camera to interchange information and so automatically control complications of exposure and how much light is emitted from the flash.

Full instructions will always be supplied with any piece of photographic equipment that you buy and, once you overcome any trepidation about entering a new field, you'll discover that today's technology has brought even the most sophisticated techniques within easy reach of the beginner.

Film

Whichever type or model of 35mm camera you use, it will take the same kind of film. The film comes in a light-tight cassette that fits into the back of the camera on the left and is threaded onto a take-up up spool on the right. Film loading is quite an easy operation once you get the hang of it, but even if you don't, many cameras today take care of the operation automatically. Most compacts are of the auto-load type and some of the newer SLRs are too. When the film is finished—after a maximum of 36 exposures—it has to be rewound back into its cassette before the camera back is opened. That too is performed automatically with most compact cameras and some SLRs. On manual models, it means no more than pressing a button and turning a crank on the camera's top.

Films come in different speeds for different needs, but for the best part of the pictures you'll be taking, a medium speed one will be fine. Speeds are measured in ISO numbers and anything between ISO 64 and ISO 200 is considered a medium-speed film. If your camera has a feature called DX-coding, it will set the film speed for you automatically as a DX-coded cassette is dropped in. Again, most compacts feature DX-coding as do many of the latest SLRs. Without that feature, it's a simple operation to twist a dial and set the speed as you load the camera.

There are three main types of 35mm film—black and white for producing prints, colour for producing prints and colour for producing slides. For commercial purposes, you will do well to avoid colour print film, since the results are difficult to sell. That leaves you with a choice of black and white prints or colour slides. As always, with any form of freelancing, look at your market to see what it requires. If most of the pictures you see in your chosen publication are in black and white, then use black and white film. If they use a lot of colour, then take colour slide film.

Black and white film is best processed by hand, rather than sending it away for trade processing the way you do colour prints or even colour slides. If you are ambitious enough to set up your own darkroom, then that's the best way to get exactly the quality and type of picture that you need. If not, try to find an amateur photographer who does have a darkroom and with whom you can work. Get black and white film trade processed and you'll be very disappointed with the results. What's worse is the fact that editors will be disappointed too.

Using the camera

Photography is both an art and a science. With the sophisticated degree of automation in today's cameras, the science is largely taken care of for you, and what isn't automated will be explained in the instruction book. What you *won't* find in any instruction book and what no amount of automation can ever achieve for you is the artistic side. That's where a few hints and tips on how to use the camera will come in handy. No one is pretending that the following pointers will turn you into a top-selling photographer. It can take many years of experience and practice to take the kind of pictures that are guaranteed to sell in their own right. But that's not what we're out to achieve. What we're doing here is looking at simple pictures that can be used to illustrate the written word. Here, then, is a ten-point plan to help you take acceptable pictures.

1. Practise holding the camera straight. It's amazing how many newcomers to photography hold the camera on a slant. So look carefully through the viewfinder to make sure that the picture you are taking is level.

2. Keep it steady. More amateur pictures are ruined by blur than by maybe any other fault. Try not to move the camera down as you press the

shutter release button. Practise holding the camera perfectly still, moving only your finger as you release the shutter. Don't jab at the button, squeeze it gently and slowly.

3.   Don't stand too far away from the subject. It's all too easy to look through a viewfinder and see only the subject you want to see right in its centre, ignoring all other detail around that subject. We all have tunnel vision to some extent, but the camera lens doesn't. It takes in *everything* that's in the viewfinder, with the result that the principal subject you were after shooting ends up much too far away. The solution is to look very carefully at the subject before you shoot. Hold the camera steady and look round all four sides of the viewfinder, taking in exactly how much of the picture area is actually being filled by your subject. So don't be afraid to move in close and really fill the viewfinder with the subject you are after, *just* the subject and nothing else *but* the subject.

4.   Don't get *too* close! You might take pictures with arms, legs and even heads chopped off. If you are using an SLR, you have no excuse because the viewfinder shows you exactly what's appearing on film. But a compact camera has a separate viewfinder which shows a slightly different view of the subject, so allow for that.

5.   When you are shooting people, try to pose them rather than shooting candidly. The sort of pictures we're talking about here can often involve people at work on, perhaps, an arts or crafts subject. So don't shoot without the subject's knowledge, or you'll probably end up with a picture of the top of the person's head. Instead, try to pose your subject so that the viewer can see his or her face and, at the same time, exactly what he or she is actually doing.

6.   If you are shooting landscapes, try to think about a few elementary laws of composition. Find an interesting aspect of the scene before you—a tree, a cottage, a church, maybe—and place it a little off-centre, rather than right in the middle of the picture. Use doorways or overhanging branches to frame the subject. Fill the foreground with a person, a gate, a rock, or some other object which will give the picture a sense of depth and scale.

7.   Keep it bright. In the UK it is all too easy to take pictures in dull weather, leading to dull, low-contrast images on film. If at all possible, wait for the sun to shine when you are shooting outdoors.

8.   Watch the way the light strikes your subject. Very often, a subject that is in shadow in the morning will be brightly lit in the afternoon, so pick

your time of day carefully. Keep in mind too that the light is better for photography when the sun is lower in the sky, during the morning or late afternoon, than when it is high around noon.

9.   Unless you are an experienced photographer, don't photograph subjects with large extra-bright or extra-dark areas in them, because that can fool the automation in many cameras and so lead to the wrong exposure.

10.   Finally, read a few good books on photography and don't be afraid to ask advice of more experienced photographers. The techniques involved aren't nearly as difficult as they might at first seem, and a little practice, together with the right sort of advice, will soon lead you towards taking the kind of pictures that can easily illustrate your written words.

Writing the captions

Whether you take the pictures yourself or get them from an outside source, they'll need some form of identification. If they are your pictures, put your name and address on the back. Use Biro, not felt-tip pen, because some of those don't dry properly on certain surfaces of paper and your writing could leave marks on the face of another print when they are packed. Better still, type the information on a separate piece of paper and attach it to the print with Sellotape.

When you write an article that contains illustrations, it is not a good idea to continually refer to specific pictures throughout your text. Instead, write a general piece that allows the editor to pick which illustrations he would like to use, then caption those pictures individually. Write your captions on a separate piece of paper, each with a number, then identify the appropriate picture with each number. Keep picture captions brief. Remember that in most publications they take up only one or two lines beneath the illustration. Just describe what's in the picture, how it is appropriate to your article and, if the picture isn't yours, include a credit for the photographer.

Picture captions, like any other form of freelance writing, follow a style. As always, look at the style in the magazine you have chosen to work for and follow it as closely as you possibly can. So much in this business can be made easy by simply giving the market what you can see it wants rather than what is merely easiest for you.

THE FICTION MARKET

**"The good ended happily, and the bad unhappily.
That is what Fiction means."**
—Oscar Wilde

You want to write a best-selling novel? Go ahead and do it. Yes, you might just crack the market and yes, there is a slim chance that you'll make a fortune, just the way all those other first-time novelists did. We've all heard the stories about the now-famous novelist whose first work was turned down by fifty different publishers before the fifty-first turned it into a best-seller. And we've heard the stories about authors who really do strike it rich the first time. But they are part of a very small minority. What you don't hear about is the thousands who fail. Despite the fact that there are a lot of books about, fiction is still a minority market. If you want to try your hand at a novel, please do. But if you want to find an easier way to make money from fiction, turn to short stories.

Even here, the market is a lot smaller than you might at first imagine. A generation ago, short story magazines and general magazines that used short stories proliferated. Today, television has taken their place. Today's "short stories" are on the box, in the form of plays, half-hour sit-coms and thriller series.

All of which is beginning to paint a rather dismal picture. But don't despair. There is still a market for short stories and, despite everything I've said above, it is a lucrative one—providing you know where to look and *providing you produce exactly the right kind of words*. The fiction market, generally speaking, is for three types of story: science fiction, short twist enders and romance. Especially romance. There's hardly a women's magazine on the market that doesn't contain a romantic story. Some are even published solely for romantic fiction, containing story after story on every page.

So your first task is to identify your target.

Finding your market

How often freelance writing comes back to this one basic precept: first find your market. It's an idea that we explored thoroughly when we were talking about writing magazine articles, and it's one that is no less important in the world of fiction. If you want to write fiction as a means to personal expression, you'll get a lot of pleasure from the exercise; but if you want to *sell* what you write, start first with the market and then write with that specific market in mind.

Go into your local newsagent and have a look through the magazines to see who is buying what. You might find some general interest magazines that need fast, easy-to-read, twist-ending stories; then there will be some American science fiction magazines, looking for material. And there will be women's magazines. This is your biggest market, and there are as many different types of women's story as there are women's magazines. Most are romance-based, but there are many different variations on the theme, as we shall see in a moment.

When you choose the magazine you are going to write for, pick one whose needs are fairly large. Unlike other types of magazine writing, the fiction market is one that relies almost exclusively on freelances, and that is something that you can exploit. Since we were talking about women's magazines, let's stay with that market for a moment. Some magazines use no more than one or perhaps two short stories per issue. Another might be published exclusively for the short story reader. Some come out monthly, others weekly. As obvious as it might sound, it's worth reminding yourself that a monthly, using one story per issue, has a need for only twelve a year; a weekly with seven per issue, needs as many as 364 stories per year. There are no prizes for guessing which is the better market!

So your first task is to pick the type of story you want to write, then to find the magazine for which you aim to write it. At that point, you start your market analysis in earnest.

Analysing the market

Buy the magazine you have chosen and read it thoroughly. Not just the short stories, but the articles too. They will give you a general idea of the type of readership at which the magazine is aimed. Every magazine has its own style. Your task is to find that style and shape your story around it. Here are twelve important points to ponder.

1. Are the short stories written in the first person (from the viewpoint of the main character), or the third person (written as though by a separate, anonymous narrator, telling a story in which he takes no active part)? Some magazines use *only* one style or the other. Don't send third-person stories if the style is obviously for first person.

2. What sex is the central character? Some accept only stories whose plots revolve around women. Others are exclusively concerned with men. Sort out which yours uses.

3. Does the magazine you've chosen use stories that are strong on description with little or no dialogue? Or do they seem to prefer a lot of dialogue and the minimum of description? Do the stories rely on a straightforward, tersely-written plot, or does the style dictate the minimum of plot, dressed up in colourful writing?

4. Do the stories always have happy endings? Or are some of them allowed to end on a downbeat?

5. Do the stories have a moral point to make or do morals seem to have no part to play? If you can spot a moral behind every story—and especially if it happens to be the *same* moral—it's a pretty fair assumption that it's a part of the magazine's style and you won't sell a story that doesn't conform.

6. How do they feel about the subject of sex? Do you want your heroine to sleep with her boyfriend on the third page? If so, you'd better check that such goings on are in order. If there's no one sleeping with anyone else anywhere in the magazine's pages, it's a good bet that such things are against their style. If you are going to introduce sex into your story, look at the way in which your magazine handles it. Do they like graphic detail, or do they go for a more subtle approach, the facts glossed over and the actual act only hinted at?

7. The same with death. If you want to kill one of your characters off half-way through the story, check that deaths are allowed and in what sort of circumstances. Once again, if no one dies in any of the stories in the magazine, it's probably because death is against their style.

8. How long are the stories? Calculate the length by the count and measure method we've already discussed in an earlier chapter. If the

longest story in the magazine is 4,000 words, you won't sell them one of 5,000. In some cases, it's no use trying to sell a story of more than 1,000 or even as little as 800 words.

9. Does the magazine favour a real-life approach to plots and characters, or does it go more for the off-beat, fantasy type of subject?

10. Are the stories told in a straight, chronological order, or is the author allowed to begin the narrative in the middle of the actual plot and tell a certain amount of the story in the form of flashbacks? There are some magazines that ban flashbacks completely.

11. What sort of class of people are featured in the stories? Every magazine editor knows his or her readership. If the magazine uses stories with which the reader is meant to identify, it's no use writing stories in which the characters move in a higher class bracket than that of the reader. In short, shop assistants don't identify with stockbrokers.

12. What sort of age are the main characters? Do the stories revolve around anyone and everyone from nine to ninety, or are the main characters in a set age group—say, sixteen to twenty-five? It's no use writing a story about a middle-aged mum for a magazine aimed at teenagers.

Going into such depth just for the sake of writing a short story might, at first sight, seem to be taking things too far. But remember what we are here for. To produce *exactly* the product required by a specific market and, in so doing, to make money from what we write. With that in mind, it's worth going to such lengths and fine-tuning your ideas accordingly. I remember writing a short story about a university graduate who became a solicitor. The story was rejected because of my misplacing of the magazine's style on class. Without altering the essentials of the plot, I changed the main character to a garage mechanic who learnt his skills at evening classes, and the story was accepted by the magazine which had originally rejected it.

If you have read your chosen magazine and there are still points about which you are unsure, simply steer your plot ideas in a different direction. Don't take chances if you are uncertain. There is a very good maxim in any form of journalistic writing that's especially worth bearing in mind when you come to write fiction. It's this: if in doubt, leave it out.

Getting ideas

Okay, you've done your research and it's time to begin writing your first short story. What you need now is a plot. One of the big mistakes is to think that plots come ready-made: the whole story presented to you in a sudden flash of inspiration. It doesn't work that way. Plots come slowly. They evolve. You start with a basic idea and build on it.

I've found that once I've had an initial idea for a story, it's a good idea to feed it into the brain and then to forget it. When I come back to the idea, perhaps an hour, sometimes a day later, other ideas will seem to have formulated themselves around the original one and the plot seems to have developed on its own. If that sounds crazy, all I can say is don't knock it until you've tried it.

Where does a short story writer get ideas in the first place? The answer to that is just about everywhere. An overheard snippet of conversation, something which has personally happened to you or a friend, newspaper reports... they're all good sources, places from which you can expand until you have a saleable plot. But enough of theory. Let's begin putting ideas into practice by looking at some of the ways that I have found short story ideas over the years.

I once read a very short paragraph in a newspaper about a woman who had kept a pile of old love letters in her dressing table drawer for years. Then one day she went out shopping, leaving some children alone in the house. When she returned, they told her they had been playing postman. They had found her pile of letters and posted one through every door in the village! The paragraph was no more than fifty words long, but it provided a good start that led to a train of thought that finished up as a very saleable little story.

I developed the character of a spinster schoolteacher who, to all outward appearances, was a dowdy, lonely woman. Everyone in her village felt sorry for her. But unbeknown to the villagers, she had a secret life with three lovers—all of whom write her letters. All goes well until one morning some local children offer to help her with her housework and she leaves them alone in the house. Based on what happened to the woman in the newspaper story, the outcome was inevitable.

Another story was sold on the basis of a conversation with a neighbour who told me how thieves had robbed a house in the next village by drawing up with a removal van and quite simply loading it with the house contents while the owners were on holiday. No one stopped the thieves because everyone thought they were part of a genuine removal company.

It sounded like a good start. In my story, though, the thieves found someone in when they called. What's more, the man said he was really moving that day and mistook the gang for the real removal company. So to get out of trouble, they went ahead with the move for the man. A couple of days later, they were all arrested—including the man from the house. It turned out *he* was a thief as well and had used the others to move all the stuff to his hideout.

See what I mean about getting an initial idea and building on it? That's how real life gave me a couple of saleable short stories. But it's also possible to pluck plots out of thin air, providing you have an active imagination and can work logically. Let's see how we might do just that.

We start by dreaming up an impossible or strange situation. Then we set out to justify it. Here goes. Let's say that a man is standing in a shoe shop, painting all the black shoes red. Right, there's a strange situation for you, now let's try to justify it.

Perhaps the man is an eccentric millionaire and the shoe shop manager hasn't stopped him because he knows from experience that the man always buys what he paints. Not bad, but not very promising. Let's try another direction.

Perhaps the man with the paintbrush *is* the manager. That sounds more promising. Now let's find a reason why he should behave so strangely. He has simply gone mad? Too simple. There's nowhere to go from there. Try this. The manager has worked for the same shop for the last twenty-five years and the boss from head office doesn't even know his name. Today is his twenty-fifth anniversary with the shop. The boss is due from head office at any moment and, for once in his life, the manager has decided to emerge from obscurity and make a name for himself—even if it means the sack.

Now we have an interesting situation and one that is worth evolving. Here's one way of doing just that. The boss arrives, sees what the manager has done and tells him to report to head office. The manager is sure that he is going to get the sack. But instead, the boss congratulates him on inventing a new fashion and promotes him. But the fact that the manager has worked in the same shop for twenty-five years probably means that he isn't the type to handle promotion. So he makes a mess of his new job and ends up back in his old one.

When I wrote, "a man is standing in a shoe shop, painting all the black shoes red" a few paragraphs back, I honestly didn't know where that idea was going to take me. What you have just read were first thoughts on the subject. They amount to nothing very special, but they do outline a plausible plot. And it all came from one initial idea.

Points about plotting

Different plots evolve differently for different markets, but there are some general points that apply to *every* kind of plot and story, whatever its market.

A plot must have a theme. This is something that can usually be summed up in a few words, and it's entirely possible that you won't even discover your theme until you are half-way through working out the plot. Once discovered, however, you must stick to it throughout the narrative. When Charles Dickens wrote *Oliver Twist*, he naturally filled a whole book. If you were to sit down and write out a synopsis of the plot, you would probably fill half-a-dozen sheets of paper. But the theme can be neatly summed up in just eleven words: Good is influenced by evil, but wins out in the end. The plot follows that theme throughout the book.

Plots are about conflict. Take a character, put him in conflict with a certain set of circumstances or, better still, with another character, and you have a sound basis for a plot. The way your central character sets out to resolve his conflict, the way he succeeds, the way he sometimes fails, these are all steps along the way that lead to the natural evolution of your story.

Plots deal with cause and effect. Nothing happens without a reason. For every cause, there is an effect and that effect then becomes a cause itself that leads to another effect . . . and so on.

A plot should have a shape. It should, in most cases, build logically towards a climax no sooner than three-quarters of the way through, then unwind, clearly enough to tie up any loose ends and quickly enough to prevent the reader from getting bored, once past the climax.

A plot should proceed logically. When something happens in a story, it should happen because of events within the narrative, *not* because the author wishes it to happen. Perhaps it's time for an illustration of plot development.

A man has a recurring dream about a beautiful girl called Louise. In his dream, she is dressed in old-fashioned clothes, holding a gun on our hero and accusing him of being unfaithful. Then she shoots him. He wakes up as the gun goes off. Eventually our hero feels he is being haunted by the girl and sets out to find if she exists. He succeeds, only to find that she is now an old woman. But she does have a granddaughter living with her who is the image of herself as a young woman. Because of her resemblance, our hero falls in love with the granddaughter. He takes her out but when he takes her home to her grandmother's house, he kisses her and they are seen by the old lady. She draws a gun, accusing him of being unfaithful and shoots him. End of plot.

It's an interesting idea, but there is something drastically wrong with that plot, and it occurs right at the end. To round off the story, the author needed our hero to be shot as in the dream. But why should an old lady shoot her granddaughter's boyfriend? Answer: because it suited the author's purpose, *not* for any logical reason that emerged from the plot. And what about that gun? Where did it come from? Why should an old lady like Louise have a loaded firearm lying around? Nothing in the plot has given her a logical reason. The gun is there at that moment for the convenience of the author, *not* for any reason contained in the plot.

Right. Let's try again. This time, with some logical explanations. It's clear that for the purposes of our plot, the hero must be shot in circumstances similar to those of his dream. So, taking that as our ending, we work backwards through the plot, making that ending logical.

Let's say that when the hero meets the granddaughter, she is distrustful. She doesn't believe his stories about dreams and it is *she* who goes to a drawer in her grandmother's house and produces the gun. It is there and loaded, she explains, because the old lady is scared of intruders. That gives its presence a logical explanation. Furthermore, it transpires that the grandmother actually killed her husband many years ago when she discovered him with another woman. Louise, as a result of this experience, is a little mad these days. The granddaughter thinks our hero has found this out and is here to turn the old lady over to the police. With the granddaughter looking so much like the young Louise, standing here holding a gun on our hero, we already have one twist to the plot, because it seems it will be the granddaughter who does the shooting. But no. That's too simple.

Our hero starts to talk his way out of trouble. In so doing, he overcomes the girl, getting the gun out of her and, in the process, she stumbles into his arms. The reader breathes a sigh of relief. Which is when Louise appears on the scene, seeing her granddaughter in the arms of our hero.

Now... We have a logical explanation of why the gun is in the house. We have a logical explanation of her slight madness and therefore the feasibility of her using the gun. And, since she caught her husband all those years ago with another woman—in a scene that must have looked a lot like the one she sees before her now—we have a logical explanation of why she might go just a little too far. She picks up the gun from where it has fallen from the girl's grasp and, with all those logical explanations behind her, what else can she do but shoot our hero?

A logical end to a far more logical plot.

Once a loser always a loser. That's another point about plotting that is worth bearing in mind. If you are writing a story about a character who is a born loser, then it's no use making him a winner in the end, just because you feel like a happy ending. If, for instance, you've built up the idea of a man who has no idea of how to handle women, he's unlikely to attract the most beautiful woman in the world by page twenty-three. That sort of thing doesn't happen in real life, and it shouldn't happen in short stories. Remember the shoe shop manager we met earlier on? He was a loser right from the start. He appeared to be a winner when he was promoted, but the way the plot evolved, he ended up right back in character again at the end.

Similarly, if you are writing a happy-go-lucky sort of story, don't give it a sad ending. Not unless you're doing so for a certain shock effect. You *can* break the rules, but you have to know them first, and you have to know *how* to break them.

Don't mix fact with fantasy. If you want to write a fantasy story about a man who learns to fly, that's fine. But your story must be shown to be fantasy right from the start. It's no use writing a factual plot about a bank robber and then having him make his getaway by flying away from the police! There are factual plots and there are fantasy plots and you should not mix one with the other.

As you work out the events of your plot, you should take things step by step, never trying to tell the whole story in one go. Once you know where you're going with your plot, arrange it to release hints, twists and parts of the story's development regularly and in rationed doses, until at least three-quarters of the way through the narrative. Here comes another example.

Charlie is an old shopkeeper, whose shop is being bought and demolished by the council to make way for a motorway. Gerry is a reporter on the local newspaper. He cares about no one but himself. When he hears about Charlie's case, he sets out to exploit the old boy, convincing him to fight the council. Right from the start we can see that Gerry doesn't really care about Charlie. All he wants is a good story for his newspaper.

There's a nice little story there, but it's badly plotted. The reader has all the facts right at the start and, if he has any sense at all, he can probably deduce for himself exactly what's going to happen in the story. And if he can work it all out for himself, why should he go on reading? Let's look at the same plot from a different angle.

Start with Charlie. State his case and make the reader feel sorry for him. Now introduce Gerry. Make him a seemingly nice guy who turns up to offer his help. Give Charlie a daughter who falls for Gerry and convinces her father, against his better nature and distrust of newspapers, that Gerry is Mr. Nice Guy, out to help them. Now, when everything is looking rosy, let your reader in on the fact that Gerry is a rotter, out to do no more than feather his own nest.

See the difference? Just as your reader is thinking that the plot is going one way, you give it a twist; introduce a new angle. You give your readers a shock, making them want to know what the outcome is going to be. You've got them hooked and now they'll read to the end.

Plots are about retribution. If a character is seen to be a baddie, then he should get his just desserts before the story is over. Similarly, if you need someone in a story to be hurt or even killed, then it's a good idea if the plot is arranged in such a way as to show that the character deserved the fate. Make him do something bad at the start—but make the action logical.

Here's an example with a ghost story, in which Simon is haunted by his dead mother. The ghost makes his life a misery, breaking up his marriage and eventually luring him to his own death. That sounds like the beginnings of a good story, but it is badly plotted. We feel sorry for Simon because his life is being made a misery. When he dies at the end, we feel disappointed, even angry. He was a nice guy, why did he have to die? What's more, why did the hauntings start in the first place? There's no logical explanation for any of it.

Look at it this way. When Simon's mother was alive, she was a really nasty piece of work. She was possessive and when he wanted to get married, she feigned illness, doing everything in her power to stop him. So he killed her. Now we have not only a good logical reason for Simon to kill his mother, we also have a logical reason for her to come back and haunt him. And because he's a murderer in the first place, we don't feel nearly so bad when he dies at the end.

Let a plot go its own way. If you've never written a short story in your life, this might sound a bit strange; if you *have* had any dealings with fiction writing, you'll understand exactly. This is something that happens to every writer and there is no reason why it won't happen to you. The fact is that there comes a point in a plot where the narrative and the characters take over. No matter what you've been planning in advance, you can often discover that the plot is taking itself in a completely new direction, one that you didn't plan at the start. Providing you remember and apply all the other rules we've examined above, then let it go. It means that having built a set of circumstances into your plot, common logic has taken over and dictated that there is only one way for the plot to take itself. To take your story in any other direction at this stage is foolish. The first time it happens to a fiction writer, it is a little frightening. But it's also very thrilling. It means that you are building a good plausible story.

Characters in the plot

No short story can exist on narrative alone. It has to be filled with people on whom that narrative is having an effect. Stories need characters, and those characters must be true to life. The first thing you'll discover with the people in your plots is that they can have a will of their own. Just as a plot can sometimes dictate its own direction, so characters can say things you never expected. Once you start to get dialogue down on paper, you'll often find your characters saying all sorts of things you never planned at the outset. That's because they are becoming, to you, real people, acting in the way real people do and saying the things that real people say.

Sit down for a moment and think about half-a-dozen of your own friends. They are each a different type of person aren't they? Perhaps one of them is a brash sort of character who never cares what he says to other people, while another is a mild type who wouldn't say a word to offend even his worst enemy. Knowing these people as you do, you can see that

Mr. Mild would never speak or act the way Mr. Brash does. Or vice versa. It should be the same with the characters in your story. Start by giving them a personality. Having established that personality, keep them in character. Don't try to make them talk or act in a way that would be outside that character. They can *try* of course, as part of the plot, but that doesn't mean they should succeed. They might *change* as part of the plot, but they need to have a logical reason for doing so.

Perhaps the best way for you, as a beginner, to organise characters is to base each on someone you know or have met. That way, you can refer the fictional character back to the real person and ask yourself if that person would act the way you need his or her fictional counterpart to behave.

This applies to all forms of fiction, even fantasy. You *must* make your characters believable. If they are not believable, the reader won't identify with them, and without that identification, you'll lose your reader.

Don't ditch your characters as soon as they have served their purpose. For a plot to be plausible a character must be seen to be in it for his or her own ends, *not* because of the author's needs. If you want a particular thing to happen in a story line, the worst crime you can commit is to just make it happen, out of the blue, with no explanation or logical back-up. The second worst crime is to introduce a new character to make it happen, then to forget that character again for the rest of the story. Give your characters reasons for being there in the first place, then give them logical reasons for doing what needs to be done.

Characters affect plot and plot affects characters. In real life, people's lives are affected by the events that surround them. Make sure that the same is true of the characters in your story. It's no use building a set of characters who are there only to push the plot along its predetermined course. If your characters are to read like real people, you must invent for them a life before and even after they appear in your story. That way you'll make them believable. This is something you can see happening in the professional world all the time. How often have you read an article in *TV Times* about the life of a soap opera character before he or she joined the series? It's all fiction of course, but it shows how the writers think a character through before their introduction to the actual plot.

The lives your characters are supposed to have led before they entered your story has shaped the way they are. By the same token, they in turn are affected by the workings of the plot. As the story finishes, your characters should be seen to have been affected by the events of the plot. However subtly, they should be seen to have changed during the course of the story. Example? Let's go back to Charlie and Gerry, the shopkeeper and reporter we met a few pages back.

Let's look at things now from the viewpoint of Charlie's daughter. Call her Joanna. The first time we see Joanna in the story is when she meets and begins to fall for Gerry. But for her to be believable, we have to give her a life of her own *before* the story began. So we start to build her character. We make her a headstrong young lady, but one who is easily influenced by others. She loves her father and wouldn't do anything consciously to hurt him, but because she is the way she is, she falls for Gerry's line and can be used by Gerry to persuade her father to see him and so start the plot rolling.

Now, because we know that the rules of plotting call for Joanna to be affected by the events of the story, we invent something that is crying out to be changed. Let's give Joanna a boyfriend. Call him Paul. And because we know that Gerry is a flashy, exciting sort of person, we make Paul just the opposite, so that it will be inevitable for Joanna to compare them. Paul is a smug sort of character, but Joanna puts up with him because she knows no different.

Having established these facts, we can now get on with the story. It was Joanna, remember, who convinced her father that Gerry was a good guy. She does that because she falls for his charm. For the same reason, she ditches Paul. Already we have a couple of characters whose lives are being changed by the workings of the plot.

About half-way through the story, Gerry turns out to be a rotter. It's best for the reader to discover this new facet of the character's nature through the experience of another character, which is where Joanna comes in again. She is out one night with him when he gets a little drunk and lets his real feelings show through. Again, Joanna is affected by the plot. She grows up a little that night, when she discovers you can't trust everyone.

Naturally, when she realizes what Gerry has been up to she gives him up. But does she go back to Paul? Not on your life. She has tasted a little adventure with Gerry and now Paul seems dull. She might not like Gerry anymore, but at least the experience has shown her there are more interesting boys in the world.

See how the character of Joanna that came in at the start of the story has subtly changed by the time she exits at the end? Because she is involved only on the sidelines of the main plot, it would have been all too easy to make her a cardboard character with no real personality, just someone there to help move the plot along, to be discarded when she had done her work. But that wouldn't have made her a real person to the reader, and because of that, the character wouldn't have worked nearly so well.

Milking ideas

A good plot is hard to come by, so if it doesn't sell to the first market you try, it can often be tailored to suit another. Here's an example that shows, not only how that theory works out in practice, but also demonstrates the way some of the other rules of plotting work out. First the plot.

Albert is a pavement artist, an old man who has worked the same pitch for years. One day, a council official tells him the road is being redeveloped and his pitch will be demolished. He decides to produce one last picture in memory of his pitch and, sitting up all night with the picture, he gets soaked in a rainstorm and catches pneumonia. He is rushed to hospital and when he leaves some time later he knows that his pitch will have been destroyed. He feels lost. He dares not go back to see what the old place looks like. When eventually he does, he gets a shock. The road is full of new shops—with the new pavements in front of them. Smooth and white pavements. Ideal for a pavement artist. He scurries off to a nearby artshop to buy a fresh box of chalks...

When I first thought that idea up, it felt like a good plot for a twist-ending 1000-word story. The magazine I sent it to didn't agree and sent it straight back. So I adapted it for a women's fiction magazine. Albert ceased to be an old man and became a young art student who worked as a pavement artist in his spare time. The story was told through the eyes of his girlfriend Gillian. In trying to give it a woman's angle, however, I ended up with a plot that was far too contrived and I didn't even bother to send it out.

Then a new women's magazine was launched, one that used a different kind of story. The stories had to have a romantic interest but the plots didn't have to be directly romantic. That was when the story took another form. Albert became an old man again and Gillian became the girl from the town hall who is sent to tell him about the redevelopment. Now, when Albert decides to draw his one last picture, he goes to Gillian and gets her to pose for him. They talk. She tells him she is about to marry, that she wants to settle down right away and have children, while her fiancé wants to travel the world for a few years first. Albert tells her to travel. She has plenty of time ahead of her to settle down.

From here the plot develops in the same way. But when Albert comes out of hospital, he is afraid to go and see his old pitch. But then he meets Gillian again. She has just returned from a trip to India with her new husband. It seems she has taken Albert's advice. Then, to round off the story, she takes him to see his old pitch and the ending is as before.

Notice how cause and effect are at work here. Gillian coming from the town hall to see Albert is the *cause* that leads to the *effect* of Albert having to leave his pitch. Albert leaving his pitch is the *cause* which leads him to the *effect* of drawing Gillian. Drawing Gillian is the *cause* which leads to the *effect* of them talking about her life. Talking about her life is the *cause* that leads to the *effect* of Albert changing her mind about her fiancé's wishes.

This time the story worked. It sold to the new magazine for which it had been precisely tailored. Unfortunately, the only trouble was that the magazine ceased publication before they could use it.

Then I heard about *Morning Story* on BBC radio each weekday morning. A contact who had had some success with this market told me they were after stories with plenty of narrative and little dialogue. Albert's story seemed ideal. One problem though: it was 4,000 words long and the BBC required between 2,150 and 2,250. Any more or less would fail to fit their 15 minute slot. So I cut the story in half and it sold, to be broadcast a few months later.

That rather lengthy example above shows how you should never give up on a good idea. Keep working at it, tuning it and adjusting it until it fits a market exactly. That's when it will sell.

By the same token, I've also had stories that have sold over and over again. Many years ago now, I wrote a twist-ending 1,000 word story about marketing men that sold to a general interest magazine. Some years after its publication, I met a man who edited an airline magazine and who was looking out for short stories. He didn't mind that they had been published elsewhere, so I showed him some of mine and he bought the marketing men story. A literary agent in Germany read it on the plane and contacted me to say he could sell it for me to a German marketing magazine. He did and I got another fee. Someone read the German marketing magazine and thought it would be good to use in a newsletter they published for heads of marketing departments. They tracked me down and paid me yet another fee for the same story. Someone who read the story in the newsletter thought it would be good to use in their Swiss chemical company's house magazine. They paid me yet again.

I honestly don't know what it is about that story, but it does illustrate yet another point about milking markets: if the plot's right, the story will just keep on selling.

Three story types

This has undoubtedly been the longest chapter in this book, primarily because it deals with one completely different, major sector of the writing market and one with which the freelance writer can earn good money. Let's finish, then, by looking very briefly at the three main types of story which sell, together with a few tips on how to increase their chances in the market place.

1. Twist enders. These are short, sharp stories that can be read in a few minutes. They are rarely more than 1,000 words long and have one thing in common: they all have a sting in the tale, an unexpected twist that leaves the reader surprised. The climax in these stories does not happen three-quarters of the way through; it happens with a bang at the end. The whole story leads up to that climax. The story actually has two plots. There is an obvious one on the surface, and another beneath the surface which you hint at and then reveal as the twist at the end. When the reader gets to the twist he or she must be surprised, yet when they think about it, they must feel that it was obvious all the way along—they just didn't see it, that's all. Your skill is in keeping it from them up until the time you finish the story. If there's one thing that sells better than a twist ending story, it's one with a double twist. Put the first twist in the penultimate paragraph, then twist the plot again and give a final one in the last paragraph. The technique practically guarantees a sale to markets that require such stories. In such a short overall length, there is little to be done about characterisation or description, so keep the stories strongly concerned with plot.

2. Science fiction. The biggest mistake that aspiring SF writers make is to think that they can abandon all the old rules of fiction writing. SF stories should be plotted and populated with characters in exactly the same way as any other type of short story, proceeding logically through the plot as you would with any conventional idea. There are two large factors, however, that set SF apart from other stories. The first is that plots are essentially about ideas, rather than characters. The characters in your plot must be as strong and as believable as ever, but they are not there as the only motivators of the plot; it's the *ideas* that do that. Time travel, anti-gravity, teleportation—there is no reason to believe or to disbelieve that any of these things will ever be possible. But they are all good, strong SF concepts on which to build plots. The other difference is that, in writing SF, you are writing about the future, whereas every other kind of short story concerns the past. That might be the genuine past of 100 years ago, or it might be the relative past of just a few minutes ago. But whatever you write about, you are dealing with events which have already happened. With SF, you are dealing mostly with events which are yet to happen. Keep all those points in mind and you'll write better science fiction stories.

3. Confessions. This is the popular name for a certain type of romantic fiction found in women's magazines. Bodice rippers is another name for them. Don't mock. They make a good market for the freelance fiction writer because there is probably more romantic fiction about than any other type. Just as SF stories are about ideas, confession stories are about emotions. The plots do not concern themselves so much with what the characters actually do, as with what the characters *feel* about what is being done to them or about what they are doing to someone else. Confessions are usually written in the first person and nearly always from the viewpoint of a girl or a woman. Usually the heroine has to be shown to be wrong about something at the start, then to learn her lesson as a result of the way things turn out in the story. Actually, it has been said, rather unkindly, that there is only *one* confession plot and, while that is a view that many might challenge, it is still very true that the said plot is one that sells and sells. It is, in fact, a plot that can be applied to many other types of fiction too, so maybe it would be appropriate to end this chapter with the one, sure-fire-success, five-point plot for confession writers. Here it is:—

(a) Put your heroine in conflict with something or someone.

(b) Have her try to resolve that conflict and fail.

(c) Take her to a crossroads in her life. One road leads to the resolving of her problems, another takes her deeper into trouble. Then make her take the *wrong* road. But don't forget to give her a good, logical reason for taking that route.

(d) Bring in an outside influence. Another person maybe, or something as inhuman as a thunderstorm. Something which forces her hand and makes her look at her problems in a new light.

(e) Have her resolve her initial conflict and learn her lesson, by way of that outside influence.

End of story!

PRESENTING YOUR WORK

"A verbal contract isn't worth the paper it's written on."
—Samuel Goldwyn

Genius, said Thomas Edison, is one per cent inspiration and ninety-nine per cent perspiration. He might just as well have been talking about freelance writing. Granted that you need the inspiration to find a subject to write about—be it fact or fiction—but once you have that idea, all else is solid graft; gathering your facts and getting them down on paper. We have already dealt with ways to get your facts and with learning about styles of writing. Now let's turn to something which appears far more mundane, but which in fact can be just as important. We're talking about presentation of your work and what to do when it's finally accepted for publication.

Laying out a manuscript

Right back at the start of this book, we looked at the tools of the trade, the theoretical ways to use typewriters. Now we're nearing the end, let's put the theory into practice and see how to set the words out on paper.

It goes without saying that all copy should be typewritten. If you can't handle that, then pay or persuade someone to do it for you. Either way, make sure first of all that your copy is double-spaced. That means leaving one complete line of space between each line of type. There is a control on all typewriters that varies this space from single spacing, when lines follow directly beneath each other, through one-and-a-half spacing and up to double and often treble spacing. If you go electronic and work on a word processor, you'll find it has a similar command that tells the printer to double-space everything.

Set your margins wider than you would for, say, a letter. A type-written manuscript should have at least one inch of space on each side of the copy. Start the first page about one-third of the way down, but start all the others a normal distance from the top.

All this space around your words is to allow a magazine's sub-editor to make his marks. He needs the space above the start of the copy to tell the printer what type-face he wants your copy set in and also the measure—the width of the column. He needs the space between the lines to insert words if necessary, so that the whole thing is clear to the printer. He needs the margins on each side, to insert other copy or remarks to the printer.

Put the page number in the top right-hand corner of your page, write "m.f." for "more follows" in the centre at the bottom of each page, and write "end" in the same position at the end of your manuscript. Start the first line full out to the width that you have set the margins. Thereafter, indent the first line of each paragraph by five spaces.Although this isn't the style for *all* magazines, it is the style for *most*, and those that differ won't mind making the changes at the subbing stage to conform with their style.

When you have finished your manuscript, take a clean sheet of paper and put the title of your feature or story in the centre, followed by your name and the number of words contained in the manuscript. Add your address and, if possible, a daytime telephone number further down the sheet. Use this as the first page of your manuscript and clip the whole lot together with a paper clip.

Before sending it off, make a final check to ensure against typing, spelling or grammatical mistakes. If you are at all unsure of your ability to spell, have your manuscript checked through by a friend. It is best, at this stage, if you send a clean manuscript, with no changes on it. But if you do find the odd small mistake here and there, you can neatly change them, using the margins and the spaces between the lines in just the way the sub-editor will. For this, there are certain printer's and editor's marks that will be of use to you (and tell your editor that you know something about his business into the bargain). You'll find an illustration of the most popularly used signs at the back of this book.

Prepare your manuscripts on plain, white A4 paper. When the work is finished, don't try to fold it into a small envelope, but send it in a full-size A4 envelope, so that it arrives uncreased. Little points like this make the presentation of your work so much better, and first impressions can often be very important in this business.

Making contact

When you send your work to an editor, you'll need some form of covering letter. The first thing to do, then, is to find out the name of the editor to whom you are submitting your work. A letter that begins *Dear Mr. Smith*, lets the editor feel that you have written this piece especially for him. One that begins *Dear Sir/Madam* gives the impression that it could have been written for anyone and that you are not actually too sure of your market. You will invariably find the name of the editor on the contents page of the magazine. On the rare occasions when an editor is not listed here, a telephone number will be, so ring up and ask the switchboard operator who the editor is *and make sure you spell the name right*. It's a good idea as well to double check the name by phone if you get the editor's name from one of the directories we were speaking about earlier. Such directories can easily be a year out of date and editors tend to swop chairs at often alarmingly frequent intervals.

The letter you write should be brief and to the point. You don't need to give a lot of waffle about the contents of your manuscript, because that should speak for itself. All you need is a letter that says something like:

Dear Mr. Smith,
I enclose a feature which I hope you will consider for publication at your normal rates. I also enclose a stamped addressed envelope for the return of my manuscript should it not meet your requirements and look forward to hearing from you in due course.
Yours sincerely,

Within that brief letter, you might have noticed two very relevant points.

The first is that you mention selling your work to the editor *at his normal rates*. This shows him first of all that you expect a fee and secondly, that you are professional enough to know the correct form when it comes to making submissions. Once again, it's a matter of correct presentation, giving an impression of professionalism that is all-important when the editor hasn't actually heard of you before. The second relevant point in that letter is the part about the stamped addressed envelope. Always enclose one if you want your work returned and, once again, if you want to show your professionalism.

The rights to sell

We have been dealing essentially with writing in this book, but we've taken in photography on the way. So we'd better consider both at this point, because each sells in a different way—even if the two are combined in a single illustrated feature.

When a magazine buys a piece of writing from you, they are essentially buying what is known as First British Serial Rights. This means that they have the right to use those words in their magazine and you must not sell the same words elsewhere. Occasionally—usually in fiction rather than features—they will build in a clause that says the rights return to you after a certain period of time. But that aside, you should not attempt to re-sell those words elsewhere in the same form.

On the other hand, you can sell them in a different form. You might find a different angle on the same subject which could be sold again to a non-competitive market. And because you've sold only the *British* serial rights, there is nothing to stop you selling the words overseas, translated into different languages.

Also, of course, you can sell the words to different *types* of markets. Words that have already sold to a magazine might, for instance, be incorporated into a book.

Pictures work differently. With each picture you take, unless you were specifically commissioned to take it, you own the copyright. You then sell the one-time reproduction rights. You can sell magazine rights, book rights, even calendar, greetings card and jig-saw puzzle rights! Ethically, of course, you should never send the same picture to two competitive markets at the same time. But there is nothing to stop you using a picture, for instance, as an illustration on photographic technique in the photo press while, at the same time, using the same shot to show a local landmark in a county magazine.

How to handle fees

The question many newcomers to freelancing ask is, How much should I charge for my work? It's a question that you should not worry yourself about, for one simple reason. When you first start out, you don't get the chance to charge for your work—you take what you are given.

That might sound a little harsh, but it isn't meant to be. The fact is that most magazines have their own standard rates, usually costed at a certain price per thousand words, plus a price per picture if you are supplying an illustrated article. An alternative to this is the magazine that pays by the published page, irrespective of the number of words and pictures that appear on that page. Either way, the rates are set and, unless you become well known to them and get yourself into a position that allows you to demand more for certain pieces of work, it's the set rates that you will be offered. It's true to say that some magazines have different rates for different contributors and that what you are offered could be less than the fee earnt by a regular and well-known writer, but by and large rates are fair and, of course, the more you sell and the more you get your name known, the better your position to negotiate a higher fee.

Speaking of negotiation, by the way, that's a word that you see quoted quite a lot in freelance directories. "Fees by negotiation," many entries say and I'm here to tell you they mean no such thing. What they *do* mean is that they don't want to put their fees in print, simply because they probably have different fees for different freelances, depending on whether or not they are known to the editor.

When your work is accepted, you should get a letter of acceptance from the magazine, offering you their set fee. Most then require you to write back and accept the fee. They might also ask you to supply an invoice. If they don't, it's because they work what's known as a self-billing invoice system which means that they actually write an invoice from you to themselves. You need offer no more paperwork then, merely collect your cheque with its remittance advice.

If you are asked to supply an invoice, there is nothing to worry about. You can buy books of invoices in office stationery shops, or you can make your own, merely typing it onto a sheet of paper or on your own headed notepaper if you have some. The invoice should contain the date, who it's from, who it is to and, for identification purposes, it should have a number. Below that, you merely detail the work carried out and the fee you require (or have been offered). Keep a carbon for your own records and send the top copy back to the magazine.

Some publishing companies actually write the invoice out for you, together with a copy for your own records. Then, it's only a matter of signing it and sending it back to accept payment.

Very few publishers pay in advance or on acceptance these days. It's far more likely that you will be paid on publication. So watch the magazine until your work appears. You will probably then be paid at the end of the following month.

Everything you earn as a freelance should be declared to the taxman, but again this is nothing to worry about. Simply keep a record of your earnings and, at the end of the tax year in April, submit those earnings to your local tax office. You will probably be getting an annual tax form to fill in anyway and you can make your declaration on that. As soon as you do that, the tax office will put you onto what's known as Schedule D. This won't affect your regular earnings from your normal employer at all, but it will mean that you'll be expected to make tax payments annually on your freelance earnings. But you don't have to pay tax on *everything* you earn. As a freelance, you will naturally have certain expenses—the cost of paper, typewriter ribbons, telephone calls, lighting and heating in the room you use to write, postage, etc. Make a note of all of these too, and keep receipts for them all. Then, when you declare your earnings, declare your expenses as well against them. Providing they are not excessive, the tax people will ask you to pay tax only on the actual profit. That's the difference between your incoming earnings and your outgoing expenses.

If you do really well, you'll have to register for VAT. Again, it's nothing to be afraid of. Despite the rumours you might have heard, VAT actually is advantageous to you. At the time of writing, you must register if you earn over £18,000 per year. Once registered, you charge an extra percentage on top of your normal fee. Again, at the time of writing, this percentage is 15 per cent and has been so for several years, but it could change. The magazines for which you write will have no objections at all to paying this extra, because they too will be VAT registered and that means they can claim it straight back from the VATman. By the same token, you must pay the extra percentage charged as VAT to the VATman. In effect, then, the magazine gets the money from the government to pay to you to give back to the government!

The advantage of being registered for VAT is that everything you then buy as part of your business can also be claimed back. So each time you buy a VATable product for the business—petrol, stationery, etc.—you too can claim back the VAT on your quarterly return. In effect, then, you are paying a percentage less for everything that you buy in connection with your writing.

VAT payments are made quarterly, but assuming you have only to deal with the ordinary inland revenue tax payments, you'll be asked for them annually—and one year behind. So for the first year, it will appear that you don't pay any tax. In the second year, you will get a demand for *that* year's payment, based on the earnings that you made in the *previous* year. Don't mix the two up, because it could get you into a terrible mess . . . and there speaks the voice of experience.

Any form of tax payment can sound complicated when you first encounter it, but in fact, once you learn the weird workings of the tax office, you'll find everything fairly straightforward. Also, contrary to popular belief, tax inspectors are extremely helpful and will always be happy to explain matters to you. The big thing to remember is not to dodge payments. Because they are sometimes slow and often far behind with their work, it's all too easy to assume they haven't noticed little old you. It's true that you might get away with tax dodging for a while, but they do know about you, because the magazine that is paying you declares its expenses every year as well—and your name and address are a part of those expenses. So they'll catch up with you in the end. And when they do, they are within their rights to ask for interest on unpaid taxes.

Dodge your tax and you'll be better off in the short term, but you might find yourself in serious trouble at the end of the day.

CONCLUSIONS

**"One of the symptoms of approaching nervous breakdown
is the belief that one's work is terribly important."**
—Bertrand Russell

So now we come to the end. Time to sit back and reflect on what you have learnt. Hopefully, you have learnt that writing for profit is a lot easier than you might have thought. Equally, I hope that you have seen that it can also be more difficult than you thought. A contradiction of terms? Not really, because the fact is that it *is* easy to earn money from your writing, once you have learnt to take time and trouble over your efforts. Often, it could be more difficult than you at first assumed to find the right market and to produce the sort of work that's needed. But once found, once you have learnt the art of matching words to requirements, everything soon falls into place.

Even so, don't assume you are immediately going to sell everything that you write. In many ways, your learning process is only just beginning. I've been writing for years, and I'm still learning. In the pages of this book, I hope I've showed you how to make a good start in freelance writing and, if you follow my directions, there is no reason at all why you should not soon start to make sales from your endeavours. But be prepared to fail. Your rejections might be few and far between, or they might come fast and furious. Either way, remember that you can learn by your rejection slips.

Often an editor will tell you what's wrong with your work. If he doesn't, if all you get is a straightforward rejection without explanation, then try to analyse your rejected work for yourself to see where you might have gone wrong. Here, then, is a ten-point plan to help you do just that. If you have been rejected, read your work through and check it out against the following points.

1. Does it suit the market?

Obviously, this is the most important question of all. Have you really understood your market's requirements and supplied its needs exactly? Or have you merely written an article for your own amusement and simply tried it out on a magazine that doesn't really use such material? Are you being too ambitious in your choice of market, simply because it is one for which you would *like* to write, rather than a less ambitious market for which you know you *can* write?

2. Is it well written and presented?

Look again at your manuscript. Is it presented in the best way? Is it type-written and is the spacing correct? How's the grammar and the spelling? If you have any doubts at all, ask a reliable friend to check it through for you.

3. Is your research good enough?

If you are presenting facts in your article, did you gather all you needed before starting out? Or did you write the article only from those facts that you personally know. If your knowledge on a chosen subject is comprehensive, then fine. But make sure the feature doesn't leave your reader with a lot of unanswered questions just because you personally don't know the answers.

4. Is it too personalised?

The mistake made by many newcomers is to make their writing too personalised—full of phrases like, *I went here* or *I did this* or *my wife did that*. Such an approach is fine if you are writing the personal experience type of feature, but if you are writing something of a more general nature, then it is far better to present your facts straight. Tell your readers how the facts of your feature will affect them not how they have already affected you.

5. Is it too localised?

Another common mistake is to assume that because a certain subject is of interest to people in your own area, it will be of equal interest to a national readership. If you are writing for the local newspaper, of course, it's different, because your words will be read by local people. But if you are writing for a national magazine or even a book, never lose sight of the fact that your words will be seen all over the country and, to a smaller extent, even around the world.

6. Is it the right length?

Most magazines work to features of a particular length. Count the words in their articles to find out what is the maximum and minimum allowed. Then make sure your feature doesn't exceed one or fall below the other. It's no use saying, "I can't write this subject in anything shorter than 4,000 words" when you can see the requirement is for no more than 1,500. If that's their requirement, that's what you have to supply and it's up to you to find a way of doing so.

7. Is it original?

Does your article truly have something original to say? Does it tell readers something they might not already know? Or are you merely telling them a few things which are new to *you*? It's all too easy to think that just because you have discovered something new, no one else knows about it. Not necessarily so. Make sure you really do have some new and interesting information to impart.

8. What about pictures?

Does your idea demand illustrations? If so, have you provided them? If you have provided them, have you given the market what it wants? Some magazines have no use at all for colour. If your market is one of those, have you sent them black and white prints? If you have sent them colour, is it in the form of prints or slides? Colour prints will be less likely to sell.

9. How are your plots?

If you're working in fiction, look at your plot again. Does it follow the rules we were discussing a few chapters back? Is the natural sequence of events logical? Does it follow the rules of cause and effect? Do the events of the plot match up to the market's real requirements?

10. Is your rejection adaptable?

If you have the bones of a good idea, but it just won't sell to one market, can it be adapted to another? For that matter, would it work *better* if it was adapted for a different market? If so, how? Which brings us back to the start. Is your idea suitable for your market, and if not, how can you change it to make it right?

All ten of those points will help you make sales as well as showing you where you might have gone wrong. To all of these, and to all the rest of the advice offered in this book, allow me to offer a few final thoughts.

The only way to start writing is to sit down and get going. If you really want to write, you'll do it—and you'll keep doing it until you succeed. I well remember a piece of advice given to me many years ago by the news editor of a newspaper for which I worked as a sub-editor. I was saying how I'd like to write a novel but didn't have the time. "If only I didn't have to come to the office everyday," I said. "If only I had enough money to sit at home and write my novel. If only . . ."

"That's all nonsense," said my news editor. "If you really wanted to write, nothing would stop you. You'd go home and start writing. All you're doing is making excuses for not starting."

And he was right. I went home that night and I started to write seriously with publication in mind. I failed dismally. I tried to write short stories and every one was rejected. It was actually years before I got one accepted, but during those years I was learning by my mistakes. Every rejection slip I received taught me something new. I kept writing until I started to sell. And the funny thing is that once I started to sell, I hardly ever stopped. It was as if all those years of rejections were little more than an apprenticeship, and having served my apprenticeship, I finally graduated into a selling writer in both fiction and features.

What I didn't have at that time, because there wasn't such a thing, was a book like this. Into the pages you have just been reading are distilled the fruits of my self-taught apprenticeship and the lessons I learnt later. If I'd had a book like this when I started out, I'd have been selling my work in months or even weeks, instead of years. Already you have a head start. So what are you waiting for? Get going. Get started. Start writing for profit.

COMMON MANUSCRIPT CORRECTION MARKS

CORRECTION REQUIRED	MARK IN COPY	MARK IN MARGIN
INSERT A WORD	The/sat on the mat _(cat above)_	cat/
CHANGE A WORD	The ~~dog~~ sat on the mat _(cat above)_	cat/
DELETE A WORD	The cat sat on ~~to~~ the mat	♂/
CHANGE A LETTER	The cat s~~e~~t on the mat _(a above)_	a/
ADD A LETTER	The ~~a~~t sat on the mat _(a above)_	a/
DELETE A LETTER	The cat sat on the ma/t	♂/
TRANSPOSE LETTERS	The c~~ta~~ sat on the mat	trs/
TRANSPOSE WORDS	The cat⌐on⌐sat⌐ the mat	trs/
CLOSE UP WORDS	The c‿at on the mat	‿
SEPARATE WORDS	The cat sat⏐on the mat	#
PUT INTO ITALICS	The <u>cat</u> sat on the mat	Italics

COMMON MANUSCRIPT CORRECTION MARKS

CORRECTION REQUIRED	MARK IN COPY	MARK IN MARGIN
TURN INTO CAPITALS	the cat sat on the mat	T/
TURN INTO LOWER CASE	The Cat sat on the mat	≢
ADD FULL STOP	The cat sat on the mat	⊙/
LEAVE UNCHANGED	The dog sat on the mat	S.T.E.T.
START NEW PARAGRAPH	When we arrived home, the cat was sitting on the mat. We turned on the fire and Tiddles began to stretch and yawn. ´Isn´t that typical of cats?´ said Rose. ´Absolutely,´ I replied, watching the animal and trying to stifle a yawn of my own.	N.P.
RUN PARAGRAPHS TOGETHER	When we arrived home, the cat was sitting on the mat. We turned on the fire and Tiddles began to stretch and yawn. ´Isn´t that typical of cats?´ said Rose. ´Absolutely,´ I replied, watching the animal and trying to stifle a yawn of my own.	RUNON